D0801750

WITHDRAWN

Foreign Investment in Canada

G
5152
.F35

JOHN FAYERWEATHER

Foreign Investment in Canada

PROSPECTS FOR NATIONAL POLICY

 International Arts and Sciences Press, Inc.
White Plains, New York

Copyright © 1973 by International Arts and Sciences Press, Inc.
901 North Broadway, White Plains, New York 10603

All rights reserved. No part of this book may be reproduced
in any form without written permission of the publisher.

Library of Congress Catalog Card Number: 73-77200

International Standard Book Number: 0-87332-041-7

Printed in the United States of America

Acknowledgments

THIS STUDY could not have been written without the valuable advice of many people. Unfortunately, anonymity requests and space preclude listing most of them. But I must start by recording my great debt to the many Canadians in government, business, labor and academic circles who helped me to understand the thinking of their countrymen.

Two people were especially helpful in my work. Carl Beigie, formerly executive director of the Private Planning Association of Canada and now of the C. D. Howe Research Institute, provided administrative support for my survey of Canadian elite attitudes and substantial advice in the present study, including a number of perceptive comments on the manuscript. Carol Seaborn of the Ottawa office of the Canadian Institute of International Affairs rendered invaluable assistance in digging up documentary material for me, especially on the historical positions of the political parties and recent Parliamentary debates. She and her associate, Bruce Thordarson, also made numerous suggestions to improve the manuscript.

Closer to home, I am indebted to the Sciafe Foundation for its financial support and to Professor Robert Hawkins for arranging for that support as part of the New York University

Multinational Corporation Project. Reviews by William Diebold and Sperry Lea of the study resulted in significant improvements. To my close associates J. Boddewyn and Ashok Kapoor I owe much in the way of long-term stimulation in our continuing studies of international business-government affairs, as well as specific comments on this manuscript. Finally, I had excellent assistance from Kathleen Alamo and Della Pruitt, who typed the drafts of the study rapidly and efficiently.

Despite all this help, the study doubtless has shortcomings for which I am solely responsible.

JOHN FAYERWEATHER

New York
February 1973

Contents

Chapter

1. A historical perspective, *3*
2. Canadian attitudes toward foreign investment, *13*
3. National decision-making processes, *72*
4. Industrial strategy, *80*
5. National policy on foreign investment, *136*

Appendix

1. A brief chronology of key events in the evolution of Canadian policy on foreign direct investment, *169*
2. Some guiding principles of good corporate behavior for subsidiaries in Canada of foreign companies (the Winters Guidelines), *175*
3. The evolution of positions on foreign investment policy in the main political parties from 1966 to 1972, *177*

Index, 197

Foreign Investment in Canada

1 A historical perspective

THE YEAR 1972 was an important turning point in the evolution of Canadian policy on direct foreign investment.* For the first time a comprehensive cabinet-level report was published on the subject. While not an official policy statement, the Gray Report was a clearer indication of government thinking than the two chief previous efforts, the 1958 Gordon Report and the 1968 Watkins Report. The Foreign Takeovers Review bill introduced in 1972 was the first piece of legislation to propose some degree of overall regulation of foreign investment. Of perhaps more fundamental importance was the start during 1972 of the far-reaching examination of Canadian industrial strategy. The legislative program proposed in early 1973 with the expanded coverage of the Foreign Investment Review bill indicated a continuation of the influences emerging during 1972 into the tenuous tenure of the new minority Liberal government.

When Herb Gray, Minister of National Revenue, was charged

---

*This study deals only with direct foreign investment, not portfolio investment. For convenience the word "direct" will not be used hereafter.

with preparing the study of foreign investment in 1970, Canadians hoped that the outcome would be a firm statement of government policy which would set a clear course for official action for some years to come. That was not the result when the Gray Report appeared. It and the proposed review bills convey some sense of official thinking and identify the specific immediate areas of government action. But many aspects of possible foreign investment policy are still being debated within the government and across the nation. The uncertainty stems particularly from the effects of the approaches to industrial strategy being considered on such matters as financing, research, exports, and production planning. And a further element of uncertainty was added by the inconclusive outcome of the 1972 national election.

The present manuscript has been prepared in an attempt to clarify the assortment of influences bearing on the future of foreign investment policy in Canada. No attempt has been made to analyze exhaustively all aspects of the subject. The fact that the Gray Report took more than five hundred pages to deal with just part of the issues discussed here indicates the impracticality of that degree of intensity of analysis in a brief study. My purpose rather is to attempt to identify the key issues, the factors influencing them, and the likely directions in which they may be resolved. While I hope there is some merit in the moderate amount of predicting I will do in subsequent pages, I have tried to place the stress on conveying an understanding of the main forces and lines of thinking at work in Canada. Predicting is a doubtful art at best, and on many points it is very hard to foresee which of several conflicting influences will shape future Canadian policy. The study is intended primarily therefore to provide as full a picture as possible of these influences and of the ways in which they interact to affect policies.

The main body of the study is devoted to three clusters of elements bearing on the evolution of national policy on foreign investment: attitudes toward foreign business, national decision-making processes, and industrial strategy. The final section will discuss the specific elements of policy on foreign investments. As an introduction to the main sections, this chapter will sketch the history of foreign investment in Canada and national policy concerning it.

The Growth of Direct Foreign Investment in Canada

In the early years of Canadian nationhood, foreign direct investment was most conspicuous in resource development, chiefly mining and pulp wood. Manufacturing operations were also getting started but on a modest scale. The population was small, and a large portion of manufactured product needs were met by imports, balancing the heavy resource exports. Through World War II the rate of growth of foreign investment was moderate, and it varied with cyclical conditions, the volume remaining essentially unchanged during the depression years. Data for all foreign investments in this period are not available. Those for U.S. investments, shown in Chart 1, indicate the pattern,

Chart 1

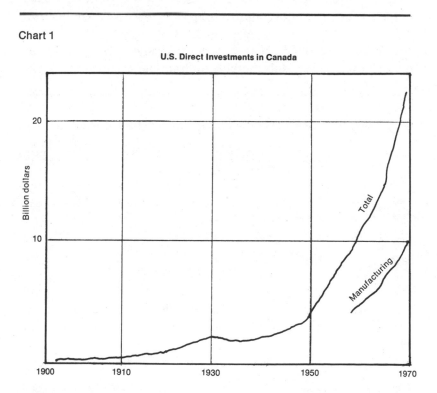

U.S. Direct Investments in Canada

SOURCE: E. R. Barlow and Ira Wender, *Foreign Investment and Taxation* (Englewood Cliffs, N.J.: Prentice-Hall, 1955), p. 11, and *Survey of Current Business,* various issues.

although in this period British investment was a substantial portion of the total.

After the war, the picture changed rapidly. Foreign firms by the hundreds set up factories in Canada to serve a strongly growing market protected by tariffs on a wide range of manufactured goods. Another motivation was the favored position of Canada as an export source for shipments to British Empire countries because of the tariff preferences. The result, as shown in Table 1, was a rapid rise in direct investment in manufacturing, especially by U.S. companies. At the same time, natural resources were attracting comparable foreign attention. Oil discoveries in Alberta brought a flood of investment. With U.S. iron deposits waning, steel producers undertook major investments to bring ore out of Labrador. And lesser ventures added to the strong growth of mining and petroleum investment shown in Table 1.

Foreign investment in manufacturing, and especially in the resource industries, substantially outran the pace of domestic

Table 1

Direct Foreign Investments in Canada (Book Value in Billions of Dollars)

	Total		Manufacturing		Petroleum		Mining/ Smelting	
	Total	U.S.	Total	U.S.	Total	U.S.	Total	U.S.
1930	$2.4	$2.0	$1.5	$1.2	$0.2	$0.1	$0.3	$0.2
1939	2.3	1.9	1.4	1.2	n.a.	n.a.	0.3	0.3
1946	2.8	2.4	1.9	1.6	0.2 (1945)	0.2 (1945)	0.4	0.3
1950	4.0	3.4	2.8	2.3	0.7 (1951)	0.7 (1951)	0.6	0.5
1954	6.8	5.8	3.9	3.1	1.5	1.4	1.1	0.9
1960	12.9	10.5	6.5	5.1	3.7	3.2	2.0	1.7
1963	15.5	12.8	7.4	6.0	4.8	4.0	2.3	2.0
1964	16.0	13.0	8.0	6.5	4.8	4.0	2.5	2.1
1965	17.4	14.9	8.8	7.3	5.2	4.2	2.6	2.2
1966	19.0	15.6	9.9	8.3	5.8	4.7	2.9	2.6
1967	20.7	17.0	10.6	9.0	6.0	4.9	3.4	2.9

SOURCE: *Canada's International Investment Position, 1926–1967,* Ottawa: Statistics Canada, Dec. 1971, pp. 108 and 124–127.

Canadian capital input. As a consequence the portion of total Canadian industry controlled by foreign firms increased notably, as shown in Table 2. In manufacturing the portion, which stood at 38 percent in 1939, rose from 43 percent in 1948 to 59 percent in 1960.[1]

Table 2

Foreign Control as a Percentage of Selected Canadian Industries, Selected Years, 1926-1963

	Percent control						
	1926	1930	1939	1948	1954	1958	1963
Manufacturing	35	36	38	43	51	57	60
Petroleum and natural gas*					69	73	74
Mining and smelting	38	47	42	40	51	60	59
Railways	3	3	3	3	2	2	2
Other utilities	20	29	26	26	8	5	4
Total of above industries	17	20	21	25	28	32	34

Petroleum and natural gas combined with mining and smelting for years 1926, 1930, 1939 and 1948.

Foreign Control of Selected Canadian Manufacturing Industries, 1963
Percentage of Capital Employed Controlled by Non-Residents

Manufacturing	Percent
Beverages	17
Rubber	97
Textiles	20
Pulp and paper	47
Agricultural machinery	50
Automobiles and parts	97
Other transportation equipment	78
Primary iron and steel	14
Electrical apparatus	77
Chemicals	78
Other	70
TOTAL	60

SOURCE: *Report of the Interdepartmental Task Force on Foreign Investment,* Government of Ontario, November 1971, p. 4.

By 1960 the great surge of relative penetration of foreign investment in the Canadian economy had reached its climax. The absolute volume of new investment in all fields has continued to grow steadily. But the rate is roughly in step with the general growth of Canadian industry. As a consequence, the portion of business controlled by foreign firms has not changed appreciably. In fact, after peaking at 60 percent in 1963, the proportion of manufacturing controlled by foreigners dropped to 57 percent in 1967, the latest official data. In petroleum the portion, which had risen from 69 percent in 1954 to 73 percent in 1960, was up only to 74 percent in 1967. Still, the degree of control was a major factor in Canadian life, especially in certain industries, as shown in Table 2.

Another important development was a change in the form of foreign investment in recent years, which has had significant effects on Canadian reactions. From 1958 to 1967, takeovers (acquisitions) of Canadian firms by foreign companies had run in the range of 60 (1958) to 93 (1960). In 1968 the number jumped sharply to 163 and has continued at that general level with only a slight drop to 130 in 1971.[2]

One more significant aspect of the investment statistics was the source of funds for expansion. In the period 1946–1960, 50 percent of the growth of foreign-controlled firms was financed by retained earnings and capital acquired in Canada. For 1960–1967 the portion rose to 59 percent.[3]

Canadian National Policies Affecting Foreign Investment

The evolution of national policies has had a major influence on the nature of foreign investment in Canada. The key elements of those policies will be outlined here, with the logics behind them and greater detail to follow in later chapters. There are three main elements of policy which appeared early and have persisted with only moderate change to the present.

The first element is an openness to foreign investment which is rare in the modern world. There have been virtually no general restrictions or even government administrative processes to impede new investors. Until the mid-fifties the general tenor of Canadian attitudes was to encourage maximum inflows of foreign capital.

Appendix 1 traces the specific items in the evolution of national policy on investment. The broad dimensions of this list tell the story. There is nothing worth noting before 1957. The

1958 Gordon Report on the Canadian economy devoted much of its space to foreign investment, setting forth the first significant expression of concern about its magnitude and effects. Its tenor was fairly mild, but the Liberal government of the time did not accord its findings official acceptance and it had little immediate impact. A general study of foreign investment was undertaken by a cabinet committee in the late 1960s, but the only visible result of its efforts was the Watkins Report produced by a task force of professors working for it. Their recommendations went a little further than the Gordon Report, though they were still very mild, e.g., an agency to collect information on foreign-owned firms and measures to prevent extraterritorial application of foreign government actions in Canada through subsidiaries. But this report was not accepted by the cabinet committee, and its recommendations had little direct impact. There have been certain specific restrictions and pressures placed on foreign investment, listed in Appendix 1, which will be discussed below. But the overall character of national policy on foreign investment remains quite open, especially in contrast to the rest of the world. The proposed bills to review takeovers and some new investments are the first significant, albeit still modest, break in this pattern.

The second element is the encouragement of maximum natural resource development in response to market demand. This goal has been furthered by government help in construction of communications and other infrastructure support and by favorable taxation. While the great natural endowment of Canada is the primary reason for the heavy foreign investment in natural resources, this official support has certainly encouraged its growth through the years.

The third element is the so-called "National Policy" of protection of secondary industry fathered by Sir John A. Macdonald, Canada's first prime minister. The National Policy took an essentially parochial view of the role of manufacturing, viewing its function as limited to the domestic market. To foster manufacturing, the government provided tariff protection, compensating for the effects of the small market size and other adverse cost factors. While this policy led only to modest foreign manufacturing investment in early years, it was, as noted above, the basis for the massive expansion of factories after

World War II, many of them U.S.-owned. But for tariffs, the firms would in many cases have either supplied Canada from U.S. plants or developed the Canada–United States market as an integrated unit with some plants in Canada and others in the United States supplying the full area.

These three elements of national policy have combined to foster foreign investment to an exceptional degree. Superimposed on their basic influence have been other elements which have changed somewhat more over time, tending to restrict or put pressures on foreign-owned firms. The first pressure to appear was motivated by the desires of Canadians to rise above the status of mere natural resource suppliers—"hewers of wood and drawers of water," as they regularly express it. There were extended struggles in the pulp and nickel industries around the turn of the century on this issue. In both cases, Canada eventually prevailed, through a combination of export taxes and other pressures, in forcing foreign companies to do a greater degree of processing of materials within Canada. In recent years this general objective has subsided somewhat in importance as Canada's manufacturing sector has grown and there have been fewer major opportunities to press the issue. Nonetheless it remains a significant theme in national policy, and wherever possible the government has applied pressure in that direction.

A second restrictive aspect has stemmed from the concern of Canadians with retaining control over certain sectors of national life. The first conspicuous event in this part of the story was the establishment of the Canadian Broadcasting Corporation in 1936, which won acceptance in large part as a means of protecting radio from foreign control. The main manifestations appeared, however, in the series of "key sector" legislative acts from 1957 to 1968 listed in Appendix 1. The basic intent of these acts was to reserve for Canadians the main areas of finance and communications media by direct restrictions on foreign ownership or other provisions which would have that effect. Canadians have generally respected property rights, so these provisions have for the most part not disturbed existing control by foreign firms. Their main effect has been to assure that there will be no further loss of control in the key sectors. In addition to the acts listed in Appendix 1, there have been some other expressions of the key sector concept, notably government intervention to block two recent takeover bids by U.S. firms. One was the 1970 Dennison Mines case in which the government acted to assure Canadian control over a major source of uranium, a resource which is regarded as vital for national interests. In the second case, the government intervened in 1971 to prevent the acquisition by a U.S. company of Home Oil Company, the only major oil producer not already under foreign control.

These two cases, along with the pattern of legislation, indicate the essence of the key sector approach to foreign investment. In contrast to the extremely open attitude toward foreign investment in general, Canadians have demonstrated a willingness to take a quite restrictive and strong approach in these particular fields. While the acts passed to date seem to have blocked out all of the main fields susceptible to the key sector approach, the coverage continued to expand somewhat, as noted in the uranium case and in the establishment of limits on future foreign ownership of investment houses in 1971 by the Ontario government.

The third element in this story is a mixture of efforts by the government to build up Canadian-owned business vis-à-vis the foreign-controlled sector. The government has clearly rejected any effort to "buy back" Canadian industry either with government funds or a combination of incentives and requirements which would result in large-scale purchase of stock in foreign-controlled firms by Canadians. However, there has been a steady expansion of moderate measures intended to increase the portion of industry owned by Canadians. The essential characteristic of the measures is to alter the competitive status moderately in favor of the Canadian-owned firms. Some of the actions impose extra costs on the foreign-owned firms, for example, the tax measures enacted in 1963 (see Appendix 1). More often the emphasis is on giving special attention to helping Canadian firms. The Industrial Development Bank and Canada Development Corporation, for example, are designed to provide financial support for Canadian ventures.

Finally, there has been a modest evolution of subtle pressures by the government to alter the behavior of foreign-owned firms to conform to Canadian interests. The most conspicuous effort in this direction was the issuance of a set of twelve "Guidelines for Good Corporate Behavior" in 1965 by Robert Winters, Minister of Trade and Commerce (see Appendix 2). Many Canadians have scoffed at the guidelines because of their voluntary character, but they do nonetheless set a standard which exerts some pressure. The pressure was subsequently reinforced by the requirement that the larger foreign-owned firms submit quarterly reports on research, exports, and other performance criteria set forth in the guidelines. The pressure is light but still there for any firm sensitive to the values of good image with the public and the government.

This is a very brief sketch of the national policies affecting foreign investment. We will return to fill in more details of the aspects which are important for the future in the final chapter. First, though, our analysis will consider the elements of attitudes, national decision-making, and industrial strategy that will largely determine the foreign investment policies.

Notes

1. *Report of the Interdepartmental Task Force on Foreign Investment* (Toronto: Government of Ontario, November 1971), p. 4, and *Foreign Direct Investment in Canada* (Ottawa: Government of Canada, 1972), p. 20.
2. *Foreign Direct Investment in Canada, op. cit.,* p. 64.
3. *Ibid.,* p. 25.

2 Canadian attitudes toward foreign investment

T HE EVOLUTION OF Canadian national policy on foreign investment is a political matter—the product of decisions by political leaders responding to their perceptions of the desires and needs of their constituents. It is appropriate therefore to start this analysis with a survey of Canadian attitudes toward foreign-owned companies. Drawing on a variety of sources, we will look at overall trends in attitudes, the quality of the attitudes, the goals underlying them, the range of attitudes among different Canadian groups, and the future outlook.

Opinion Trends

One of the few clear-cut facts in the current Canadian picture is the strong trend in recent years toward less favorable views of foreign investment. The trend is conspicuously evident in a flood of written and spoken opinions. Results of two surveys suffice to provide quantitative confirmation. Gallup polls record the following change over eight years in responses to the question of whether Canadians feel they should have more U.S. capital.[1]

	Enough U.S. capital	Want more	No opinion
1964	46%	33%	21%
1967	60%	24%	16%
1970	62%	25%	13%
1972	67%	22%	11%

Results of annual surveys of 5,000 Canadians reported by J. Alex Murray and Mary C. Gerace show a steady increase in adverse opinions of U.S. investment.[2]

Question: "Is U.S. ownership of Canadian companies good or bad for our economy?"

	Bad (%)	Good (%)	Qualified, both good and bad (%)	No opinion (%)
1969	34	43	7	16
1970	41	38	13	8
1971	44	39	7	10
1972	47	38	7	8

The trend in attitudes cannot be directly correlated with changes in the actual foreign investment situation. Already in 1948 foreign firms controlled some 43 percent of Canadian manufacturing but there was virtually no concern on this account and the government was energetically encouraging a greater inflow of foreign capital. It is hard to explain by any logic of size that the present roughly 60 percent is different enough from 43 percent to account for the very great rise in concern about foreign investment. The magnitude of investment may not in any case be the critical factor in people's attitudes. Comparative studies of attitudes of elites that I have made in Britain, Canada, and France show the views in all three countries to be quite similar.[3] Since foreign companies control less than 10 percent of manufacturing in Britain and

France compared to about 60 percent in Canada, these responses suggest that attitudes toward foreign investment are only partially due to its magnitude.

The degree of control of Canadian manufacturing by foreign firms having risen to 57 percent already in 1958, the further increase since that time, as noted in Chapter 1, has been very minor. Yet the rise in public interest has largely developed since 1958. By the mid-1950s astute observers were already conscious of virtually all of the significant adverse effects which are being publicly decried today. An article in the Toronto *Globe and Mail* vividly demonstrated this by quoting key passages from the Gray Report side by side with quotations in essentially the same vein from a speech by MP George Drew in 1956.[4] The Gordon Report in 1958 enunciated much the same views but it received little favorable reaction from either the government or the general public at that time.

In light of the minor changes during the past fifteen or so years in the degree of foreign industrial control and in the understanding by leading people of the impact of that control, we must attribute the trend in public attitudes to other factors. In part the evolution may simply be an indication of the time required to communicate a fairly complex subject to the people and to arouse their interest in it. While the issues surrounding foreign investment occasionally make good headlines, by and large they are rather subtle, sophisticated matters, not readily appreciated by the general public or even elites not closely associated with them. For a large portion of Canadians, practical experience with foreign-owned firms either as consumers or employees has been essentially satisfactory, so there has been little pragmatic basis for arousing concern. One highly significant observation from a comprehensive survey of attitudes in an Ontario city with a substantial number of foreign-owned companies was that, despite some strong individual views, the majority of the citizens were essentially apathetic about the foreign investment question.[5]

A second quite visible factor which may have contributed to the recent rise of adverse views is the effect of U.S. economic policies, reinforced to some degree by reaction to other U.S. affairs such as the Vietnam War and racial problems. Certain economic policies have had potentially severe implications for

Canada, notably the U.S. efforts to correct the balance of payments deficit: the Interest Equalization Tax, the direct investment restraints, the 10 percent surcharge on imports imposed on August 15, 1971, and the creation of the Domestic International Sales Corporation (DISC) in 1971 to foster U.S. exports by tax deferrals for half of the export profits. Canadians perceive DISC as a major threat since it would encourage U.S. companies to substitute exports from the United States for production in Canada. Dire consequences, such as the prospect of half of Canadian plants closing, have been voiced by politicians, though most people speak in terms of more moderate impact.[6] The extent of worry about DISC is indicated by the fact that it was mentioned in 49 of the 109 days of House of Commons sessions from December 1, 1971 to July 7, 1972. The potentials of injury to Canada by these U.S. economic actions have not actually been experienced because of exemptions from the initial balance of payments measures, the brevity of the surcharge, and the short history of DISC. Furthermore, Canadians have the capability of taking actions to offset many of the things the United States may do. Indeed, in introducing the 1972 budget, Minister of Finance Turner indicated that trade policies of other countries (including, clearly, DISC) were an important consideration in the proposed corporate tax cuts.[7] But there is a cost to Canadians for such responses and they do not eliminate the basic sense of vulnerability. The recent U.S. government moves, along with assorted lesser actions, therefore have impressed strongly on Canadians the ability of the United States to hurt the Canadian economy, and this consciousness undoubtedly has rubbed off on attitudes toward foreign investment.

Third, there have been some instances of rather hard-handed action by the U.S. government which have aggravated anti-American sentiment. The manner in which former Secretary of the Treasury John Connally handled negotiations of various economic problems in 1972 aroused much adverse comment in the Canadian press. While the facts have not been publicly documented, Canadian public opinion has been convinced by the writings of influential people that the U.S. government intervened with exceptional pressure on behalf of U.S. companies against two Canadian government actions.[8] While these items are rather small in the vast range of quite amicable relations between Canadians and U.S. businessmen and government officials, they receive major press attention and have a quite large effect on opinion formation.

A fourth line of explanation suggested during my interviews is more subtle but perhaps just as important. It relates to the general approach of Canadians to internal affairs. Traditionally, it is said, government activities went along from year to year with little reexamination or innovation. As one official put it bluntly, "Life was dull." Then in the 1960s an awakening process gained momentum and a number of matters came under scrutiny, ranging from constitutional reform to economic policies, including regional development, science, and the like. As these reviews of internal matters proceeded, foreign investment emerged in the minds of government officials and others as more and more important for two reasons: first, it was identified as a contributing factor in many of the internal issues being examined, and second, its character was a complication in many of the solutions being proposed. Thus, while there was nothing new in the facts of foreign investment, its implications were now being expressed very directly and personally in the responsibilities of many people who previously had been unconcerned with it.

The Quality of the Attitudes

The polls cited in the previous section might lead one to believe that in a national referendum Canadians would vote to stop further foreign investment. But that impression is quite misleading. The polls accurately reflect the *feelings* of Canadians when presented with the problem without explicitly stating either the costs or the alternatives. Most Canadians would indeed rather not have more foreign investment. But taken by itself that opinion tells us no more than knowing that most Canadians are opposed to pollution tells us about pollution regulation programs. To understand the true quality of the attitudes, therefore, one must look at the perceptions of Canadians as to the effects of foreign investment and its importance compared to interrelated matters.

Table 3

Canadian Attitudes on Effects of Activities of Foreign Companies

	Favorable		Neutral	Unfavorable	
	2	3	4	5	6
Overall					
Elite		B	G L	U	
General		B	P H M C A	W T	S
Culture					
Elite		B L	G U		
General		H C	B T P M A	W	S
Economic, Overall					
Elite		B	G L	U	
General		B	C P H	T W A M	S
Payments to parent					
Elite			B L G	U	
General			S B P H W	T C A	M
Control					
Elite				B	G L U
General				B C W A	P H M T S

SOURCE: John Fayerweather, Canadian attitude surveys.

Notes on Table 3

QUESTIONS

1. In your opinion, what is the overall effect on Canada of the activities of foreign companies in Canada? Good = 1, Bad = 7.
2. Are the changes in way of life referred to in Question 13 good or bad? (Q. 13 referred to influence of foreign firms on Canadian way of life.)
3. What do you believe is the net economic result of the operations of foreign companies in Canada? Give more than take. Take more than give.
4. In relation to their economic contributions, the dividends, royalties, and other payments which foreign companies receive from their operations in Canada are: Too small. Too large.
5. What will be the result for Canada if foreign companies have greater control over policy decisions in Canadian industry? Good. Bad.

SYMBOLS

Elite:
B   Heads of business firms
G   Permanent government officials
L   Members of Parliament
U   Labor unions officers

General:
B   Businessmen
P   Professionals (lawyers, doctors, etc.)
M   Merchants
C   White-collar workers and supervisors
W   Blue-collar workers
T   Teachers
S   Students
A   Agriculturalists
H   Housewives
R   Retired

A broad picture of the perceived effects of foreign investment is provided by a recent attitude study. In late 1971 I made a survey of four elite groups (members of Parliament, permanent government officials, heads of business firms, and labor union leaders).[9] A related survey of a sample of the general public was made for me in early 1972 by a private organization. The results of the latter survey were not entirely satisfactory, as there was a poor response from low income groups. However, the data from both surveys, shown in Table 3, confirm a quite consistent pattern of attitudes on the three main

types of effects of foreign firms on Canada. The judgment of
the cultural impact is essentially neutral; the economic effects,
both overall and on the balance of payments, are considered
somewhat on the negative side; and the loss of control of
national affairs is viewed as quite adverse.

This pattern may be considered with other evidence on the
subject. Murray and Gerace report that those who were favorable to foreign investment most often mentioned its economic
contributions.[10] Those with adverse views based them most often
on the loss of control of national affairs. Both the Gordon and
Watkins reports basically judged that foreign investment had
made a net economic contribution, their negative views being
aimed most heavily at the political cost.[11] The Gray Report
observes that "such studies as have been done by others—and
they involve many qualifications—tend to suggest that the overall impact of foreign direct investment on economic activity has
had a moderately favourable effect."[12] Its economic criticisms
are directed at specific multinational firm actions (e.g., procurement and exports) more than their total performance, and
again the emphasis is on the control aspect.

This evidence fits a generally perceived Canadian view that
there is a trade-off between economic benefits of foreign investment and loss of control of national affairs. Thus in the ongoing national debate on the foreign investment issue, economic
consequences of nationalistic policies constantly intrude. To
convey a sense of this pervasive perception, it is useful to inject
a few quotations from people who cover quite a span in the attitude spectrum.

Max Saltsman of the New Democratic Party, speaking to a
group from the Maritime provinces, observed: "Those of us in
Canada, such as central Ontario, that have industry can afford
to be selective, those like you who have not can hardly afford
the *luxury of nationalism*" (emphasis added).[13] Raymond Rock,
an independently minded Conservative (formerly Liberal) MP
from Quebec, speaking on the failure of the government to
solve unemployment, criticized the Liberals and NDP for making Canadian nationalism "anti-American and anti-foreign investment" and especially the extreme nationalists "who scare
the hell out of the industrialists who want to expand their industries in Canada . . . whether they are foreign owned, American

or even Canadian, and add to the causes of unemployment."[14] He also quoted the view of another prominent Canadian in considering the economic outlook: "John Deutsch, former chairman of the Economic Council of Canada, feels that there is no country where the blind furies of nationalism could be more dangerous than Canada in the 1970's."

Prime Minister Trudeau, defending the decision to go no further than the takeover review system in 1972, said that this was the strongest step Canada could afford to take then, although "in the future other trade-offs will be possible and other decisions made. The alternative would be to have a fall in our standard of living, less jobs for Canadians and certainly great fights between the provincial governments and the federal government."[15] NDP leader David Lewis states: "We are concerned about this [foreign investment] not for any reason of arid nationalism but for very concrete reasons affecting Canadian jobs and the shape not only of our economic destiny but of our national identity and culture as well."[16]

One could also give many quotations which explicitly deal with the economic cost of nationalistic constraints on foreign investment. But this assortment of statements illustrates more vividly the acute and pervasive consciousness of the issue which surfaces in quite varied people and different contexts. The policy positions of Saltsman, Rock, Deutsch, Trudeau, and Lewis are quite different. But each is relating to the common belief that nationalism has a cost and that the cost must either be justified or avoided.

The perception that greater independence through reduction of foreign investment would carry an economic cost leads naturally to putting that choice directly to the people. Unfortunately, opinion studies of this nature are not very satisfactory because they pose hypothetical choices to which people may not respond realistically. Still, such efforts have been made and the results provide some indicator of reactions.

My surveys contribute one type of information on this point. One question in the survey asked for opinions on the Canadian-U.S. Automotive Trade Agreement. The details of the agreement will be described further in Chapter 4. Suffice it at this point to say that it has had economic benefits for Canada with an offsetting loss in a shift in the locus of decisions in the industry from Canada to the U.S. headquarters of the companies. The respondents in the survey were asked to indicate their appraisal of this trade-off. The results may well have been distorted because it happened that just before the survey was mailed, the whole issue of the Automotive Trade Agreement broke into the news and the benefits to Canada were being loudly proclaimed in reaction to U.S. efforts to modify the deal. The results shown in Table 4 are therefore not as informative as they might have been, but they do give some suggestions as to how Canadians react to the trade-off.

Table 4

Attitudes Toward Canadian-U.S. Automotive Trade Agreement

Question:
According to a recent study the Automotive Trade Agreement has had these significant results on Ford operations: (1) economic benefits for Canada including cost-price reductions of at least $100 per car on affected models, and (2) more centralization of control of decisions in the U.S. headquarters because of integration of Canadian and U.S. production operations, thus reducing the independence of Ford-Canada and shifting some staff functions from Canada to the United States. In light of these types of changes, do you think the agreement is a good or bad thing for Canada?

                1 = Good for Canada   7 = Bad for Canada

Elite survey	Average score		Average score
National legislators	3.3	Labor leaders	3.2
Government officials	3.2	Heads of firms	2.8
General population survey			
Occupation			
Business managers	3.8	Commercial	5.3
Farmers	4.1	Teachers	5.3
Professionals	4.7	Blue collar	5.4
Housewives	4.9	Retired	5.4
White collar	5.2	Students	5.5
Region			
Ontario	4.5	British Columbia	5.3
Quebec	4.7	Prairies	5.4
Maritimes	5.0		

SOURCE: John Fayerweather, Canadian attitude surveys.

The most striking fact is the wide gap between the essentially favorable view of the elites and the clearly negative view from the general survey. Since the appraisal of the overall effects of foreign firms was only slightly less favorable for the general group than for the elites (Table 3), this gap is significant. The most likely explanation would seem to be that the elites were more conscious of the balance of payments and employment benefits than the general public. Another explanation offered to the author by a member of the Canadian elite is that knowledgeable people feel that the switch of functions from Ford of Canada to Ford in Detroit represented in reality a very small change in the real locus of control. In any case, the elite data would not seem to provide useful evidence on the cost-control issue.

The data from the general survey seem more informative. There is no apparent consideration outside of the control issue stated in the question to influence the opinions so clearly to the negative side. Assuming some external influence from public discussion of the balance of payments and job effects, we must judge that the stated loss-of-control effect exerted a strong negative pull on the attitudes of the respondents. The conclusion is given further force from the data broken down by region. While Ontario people are not generally the most positive toward foreign firms (see p. 38), they were the most favorable toward the Auto Pact, presumably because they were closer to the job aspects and more informed about its general impact. The people more distant from the industry have the most clearly negative reactions. Thus the indications are that, faced with a concrete situation in which they might find $100 in their pockets gained at the cost of surrendering a piece of control over their industry, the majority of Canadians in this survey would give up the $100.

Some further indications of Canadian feelings on the trade-off between economic benefits and control are provided by two other surveys. One general survey in 1971 asked if people would accept a lower standard of living in order to keep further foreign investment out of Canada. The "nos" were slightly more numerous than the "yeses" (46.6 percent vs. 43.9 percent).[17] In another survey, MP Max Saltsman found that 95 percent of his constituents wanted more independence but with no loss of standard of living.[18]

These results indicate the difficulty of determining clearly

Table 5

Criteria for Evaluating Foreign Firms: Computed Rank Order Score

1 = Most Important

Effects in Canada	Elite					General								
	Members of Parliament	Permanent govt. officials	Labor union officers	Company heads	Aver.	Business-men	Merchants	White-collar workers	Blue-collar workers	Profes-sionals	Teachers	Students	Farmers	Aver.
Control over national affairs	1.0	1.0	1.1	1.2	1.0	1.0	1.1	1.2	1.4	1.0	1.0	1.5	1.0	1.1
Effect on national income	1.5	1.4	1.0	1.2	1.2	1.2	1.0	1.3	1.0	1.6	1.1	1.1	1.6	1.2
Role of Canada in the world	1.5	1.4	1.0	1.2	1.2	1.8	1.4	1.3	1.0	2.6	1.9	1.6	2.2	1.6
Effects on balance of payments	1.1	1.6	1.8	1.1	1.3	1.3	2.3	1.6	1.3	1.5	1.1	1.1	1.8	1.3
Benefits for workers	1.8	1.6	1.0	1.3	1.3	1.2	1.0	1.0	1.0	1.3	1.0	1.0	1.5	1.0
Opportunities for managers	1.5	1.9	1.9	1.0	1.5	1.2	1.6	1.3	2.7	1.6	1.4	2.1	2.2	1.4
Opportunities for investors	2.1	2.1	1.9	1.2	1.7	1.8	1.9	1.1	1.3	2.1	1.2	2.1	1.8	1.5
Changes in way of life	2.1	2.3	2.2	2.4	2.1	2.2	2.1	2.3	2.4	2.4	2.1	2.2	2.2	2.2

BASIS   Question: "How important should the following considerations be in judging the value of foreign companies operating in Canada?" Major importance = 1; Minor = 7.

In the above table the considerations with the lowest average score for each group were given the rank of 1.0. The ranks of the other criteria are the sum of 1.0 plus the difference between their scores and those of the top ranked criteria for the group.

the degree of sacrifice Canadians are willing to accept as a cost of independence. Per capita income is now 25 percent less in Canada than in the United States. Thus most Canadians are conscious that they already are paying a high price for independence. Without any pretense at precision, one can simply impute from the surveys and other impressions that it is doubtful whether a majority of Canadians are prepared today to accept *significant* additional economic sacrifices to reduce the role of foreign firms, though minor costs may be acceptable.

The economic-vs.-control effects of foreign investment can be presented as a concisely stated trade-off. But the realities of these two major aspects of the impact of foreign investment are quite diverse, as will be observed in the discussion of industrial strategy in Chapter 4. To assess the quality of the Canadian attitudes one must therefore know where the various elements fall in the priority scales of the people. Two types of information are useful for this purpose.

First, my surveys of Canadian attitudes on foreign firms give a ranking of importance of various effects of foreign firms on Canadian life. The data in Table 5 indicate that the control and economic effects rank about equally high. In fact, only the last item, the cultural impact, is clearly of subordinate importance, with the effect on managers and investors relatively low. Statistically, the other five are all close enough so that they are essentially of the same rank. Thus these data indicate that in thinking about the foreign investment issue, the control impact and the economic consequences—including national income, balance of payments, and employment—are all of major concern.

The second type of information places the foreign investment issue in perspective in relation to other matters of national interest. The results of two Gallup polls reporting the "main worry" of Canadians indicate their priorities:[19]

	1966	1972
Employment	7%	41%
The economy	35%	14%
U.S. control	3%	8%

These data confirm the rise in concern over foreign investment already discussed. But most strongly they place the question as clearly subordinate to economic issues. The change among the latter is also interesting and we shall return to it in Chapter 4.

Another gauge of priorities is provided by the following data from a nationwide survey made by the Toronto *Daily Star* just before the 1972 election to determine what issues the people felt were of importance (1) for the federal government to do something about, and (2) in deciding for whom to vote.[20]

	First Question		Second Question	
	First mention (%)	All mention (%)	First mention (%)	All mention (%)
Unemployment	48	63	34	55
Inflation, cost of living	8	26	8	37
Taxes	6	19	10	26
Too much welfare	3	12	2	6
More help for elderly	4	11	4	12
Pollution	2	8	2	10
Farm problems	3	7	3	6
Abuse of unemployment insurance	2	4	1	1
Quebec's position in Canada	2	4	6	13
Economic growth	1	4	2	5
Youth	1	4	1	7
Education	1	4	–	2
Drug problem	1	4	1	5
American investment	1	3	2	8
The economy	1	3	3	5

Foreign investment is far down on the list, with general economic issues again dominant.

A third indicator is a report of a series of interviews by Peter Regenstreiff with voters prior to the election.[21] The report conveys a picture of the questions which were on the minds of Canadians. The dominant elements were the personalities of the main candidates and the economic issues of employment and inflation. Foreign investment is not even mentioned in the report.

Departing from factual studies, we may broaden the information input here to include the overall image of the importance of the foreign investment question evident in the 1972 campaign. The overwhelming impression is of its negligible role. This fact was due in part to the lack of significant differences between the two major parties, a matter which will be discussed later. But in large part it confirms the relatively low priority given to the subject. I was informed in my interviews that the decisions of the major parties not to emphasize the issue were based on their private polls which showed that the subject had little voter appeal as compared to unemployment, inflation, etc. —the same picture as the *Daily Star* poll.

In a few cases, candidates for parliamentary seats did try to make foreign control an issue. The most notable instance was the contest between Liberal Mel Hurtig, co-chairman of the Committee for an Independent Canada, which will be described later in this chapter, and Marcel Lambert, the financial expert of the Conservative Party in Edmonton, Alberta. Hurtig pushed the nationalistic CIC program hard while Lambert labeled it as "retrogressive" and basically ignored the issue.[22] Lambert won by almost 9,000 votes compared to about 2,000 in the 1968 election. The greater margin was doubtless largely part of the general switch away from Trudeau. But it at least indicated that the strong nationalistic program had no compensating appeal. In the Don Valley district of Toronto both major candidates—Liberal incumbent Robert Kaplan and Conservative James Gillies—tried to elevate the issue to some importance as both believed in greater efforts along nationalistic lines. But they found a discouraging lack of public interest and therefore did not press the issue.[23] The New Democratic Party made periodic efforts to push the foreign investment question to the fore, but it also got little response. By comparison the NDP apparently was highly successful with its basic theme, the "corporate welfare bums," charging that business was reaping rewards of assorted government handouts while the people suffered from unemployment, inflation, and other economic troubles.

This evidence does not mean that foreign investment was out of the minds of candidates or voters. A survey of a sample of candidates late in the campaign showed the following percentages rating the foreign investment issue as very serious: NDP— 98 percent, Liberals—78 percent, and Conservatives—54 percent.[24] The same *Daily Star* survey of voters quoted above

showed also that 43 percent favored restrictions on U.S. investments.

The conclusion to be drawn from the evidence is rather that
in the crunch Canadians are far more concerned with the economic problems immediately affecting their lives than the quite
nebulous question of foreign control. Since actions to deal with
the latter are perceived as having possibly adverse economic
effects, Canadians are generally hesitant about them. Thus,
while the desires of many Canadians to limit foreign investment
and reduce the degree of control it exerts are real, their quality
as a factor in actual decisions is strongly moderated both by
their ranking of the problem beside other issues and the effect of
those issues on it. The apparent outcome is that the force of
the attitudes is rather moderate in the nation as a whole.

The Quest for National Identity

While this assortment of facts about Canadian reactions to
various effects of foreign investment gives us some picture of
the components of attitudes, it does not convey a full sense of
the attitudes currently motivating the people in the evolution of
policy. To get a better feel for those motivations, one must look
at a deeper philosophical level of Canadian thinking. The differences in attitudes on foreign investment and the changes in
those attitudes over time are due in no small part to the difficulty
Canadians experience in defining the goals of their nationalism.
Virtually all Canadians will agree that they wish to preserve the
"national identity" of Canada. But what does that mean? There
are a variety of views based on differences in opinions as to
what is desirable and what is feasible.

The feasibility aspect would appear to be of prime importance for the future evolution of attitudes and national policy.
Depending upon whose assessment is correct, there may be virtually no scope for Canadian identity, or the opportunities may
be quite substantial. The major element in this story, of course,
is the great size of the United States and the tremendous influence it exerts on every aspect of Canadian life and affairs.

An excellent presentation of the thinking of those who regard the preservation of national identity as hopeless is found in George Grant's *Lament for a Nation*.[25] Grant's scholarly treatise develops at some length the nature of the impact of the United States on Canada and the evolution of the response to that impact. His conclusions are based on two main points. First, he observes that the basic purpose of life is consumption and that the benefits for consumption from economic integration with the United States are so overwhelming that the border is an anachronism.[26] Second, he argues that there is virtually nothing unique about Canada in its culture or other characteristics, and therefore its preservation as a nation is not only impractical but not even worthwhile.[27]

Grant foresees a considerable passage of time before these basic forces will deliver the final blow to Canadian identity: "Canada has ceased to be a nation but its formal political existence will not end quickly."[28] Inertia, the political decision-making process, and, ironically, U.S. resistance to absorption of Canada particularly because of the French-Canadian problem will, he anticipates, defer for many years full political union with the United States. But Grant's basic message to Canadians is that they are simply deluding themselves today by any talk of national identity.

Some Canadians given to intellectualizing concur in Grant's assessment. Many others who are pragmatically oriented live according to it, accepting without reservation the high degree of Americanization of Canadian life and the powerful influence of the United States on economic and political affairs. But the majority of Canadians are not prepared to accept the inevitability of the demise of their nation. Their determination to preserve some degree of national identity is a striking example of the powerful inner motivations of the universally experienced psychology of nationalism. But the definition of a viable national identity is an uncertain and difficult challenge for these people in the context defined by Grant.

The preservation of Canadian culture as a foundation for national identity has great appeal. In the French-Canadian case, the people have before them a notable demonstration of the strong nationalism which a group can maintain even while it is a part of a broader national state. And despite the high degree of Americanization, there are distinctive elements of Anglo-

Canadian culture not only in formal institutions but in basic ways of life (e.g., the pace of life and the manner in which people interact).

But the preservation of these differences and their relevance for national identity are highly uncertain. The pervasive force of Americanization cannot be avoided. Two facets suffice to indicate its impact. First, there is the broad communication through U.S. magazines and television, which dominates the cultural consumption of the general public. The second is the massive input of U.S. culture in the Canadian educational system, both in textbooks at all levels and in the professional ranks of higher education. Some recent data have provided striking evidence on the latter count. For example, a survey at Simon Fraser University in 1967–1968 showed that 68 percent of the professors were not Canadian citizens.[29] Some 75 percent of professors recruited by all universities in 1971–1972 were non-Canadian.[30] An impressive indication of the effect of this condition was a report that a number of Canadian students, in writing papers for a particular course, used the terms "my," "ours," and "us" when they were referring to the United States.[31]

Canadians have responded quite vigorously in the cultural area, indicating that this is an aspect of national identity which they are prepared to protect and for which they will pay a price. There are already regulatory measures governing such matters as the percentage of radio and television time which must be devoted to contents of Canadian origin. The mandatory character of such measures indicates that they carry a cost. That point is confirmed by the evidence of opposing pressures, for example, in the decision of the government-owned CBC to increase the American content of its schedule in 1968–1969 to increase revenues and please its affiliates.

It is hard to tell at this point whether the present pattern of actions will be maintained as a permanent commitment of Canadians to preserve national cultural identity, or whether it represents a series of rearguard actions providing immediate outlets for the nationalistic desires of people, fated ultimately to succumb to long-term evolution of a North American continental culture. The only point which does seem clear is that interest in preserving cultural identity is strong, and it is significant not only in itself but also because it provides an outlet for nationalistic desires which in some respects are more practical for Canadians than economic identity. U.S. forces, notably government and industry, exert far less direct influence in Canadian cultural affairs than in economic decisions. Thus at an institutional level the feasibility of exerting national control to protect the culture is high.

But cultural identity does not seem to be sufficient to satisfy most Canadians. The dominant desire is for control over national affairs. This is altogether natural because the maintenance of control over the destiny of one's own society is fundamental to the psychology of nationalism. Its meaning in the current search for national identity in Canada is far from certain, however.

As a starting point in exploring this topic, it is useful to examine the thinking of Prime Minister Trudeau. As an articulate intellectual, Trudeau has committed much basic thinking to writing over the past twenty years or so. He is a man of sharp analytical faculties and strong views, willing, perhaps anxious, to speak in opposition to major social groups. In earlier years in Quebec he was outspoken in criticism both of the ruling establishment and the separatists. While the 1972 election results make his political future uncertain, he is for the moment the Liberal leader, and because of his strong personality, his views are a significant element in the Canadian scene.

The most important point for the present analysis is that Trudeau basically does not believe in nationalism. His writings are replete with criticisms of nationalism often approaching emotional castigation.[32] While many of these comments are specifically directed at separatist nationalism in Quebec, his opinions deal with nationalism in general and are based on sufficient national and even international experience so that one must assume that this is a matter of basic philosophy. The thrust of his thinking lies in the direction of the rational structuring of economic and political organization. Essentially he feels that nationalism will in time become obsolete, being replaced by functionalism, a greater degree of rational rather than emotional motivation and direction of national action. His own inclination is to move as rapidly as possible in this direction.[33]

Working from this philosophical base, Trudeau functions

within the realities of decisions which must be made and of the political context to which they must relate. The following quotation would appear to capture the key elements in his outlook on the foreign investment situation:

> I don't worry over something which is somewhat inevitable, and I think the problem of economic domination is somewhat inevitable, not only of the United States over Canada but perhaps over countries of Europe as well. . . . These are facts of life, and they don't worry me. I would want to make sure that this economic presence does not result as I say in a real weakening of our national identity. I use that general expression too. The way in which I do that is to try and balance the benefits against the disadvantages. It is obvious if we keep out capital and keep out technology, we won't be able to develop our resources and we would have to cut our standard of consumption in order to generate the savings to invest ourselves and so on. . . . Each country wants to keep its identity or its sovereignty, to speak in legal terms. It has to instantly make assessments, and when we make assessments it is to try and select those areas which are important for our independence, for our identity.[34]

One would sense from this that Trudeau stands apart from the great body of his countrymen in having little personal attachment to nationalism. Logically his thinking would appear to run towards pragmatic determinations as to whether national or continental or worldwide approaches were most beneficial from a practical standpoint on matters affecting human welfare. However, there are three constraints on this pure functionalist approach. First, Trudeau is not only an astute politician, sensitive to the attitudes among his people, but scattered through his writings one senses a sympathy with the emotional value of nationalism to most people. While he, as an intellectual, may find no satisfaction in it, he sees that the satisfactions, for example of cultural nationalism, are important to society as a whole.[35] Second, one sees in the quotation above, as well as in other writings, a personal adherence to the political concept of the nation which he would work to preserve. It would seem that the support of political identity for a nation is important enough to him so that he will defend the merits of special measures to retain control of those institutions which are important for that purpose, notably the financial system and major communications media of the country.

Third, Trudeau believes so strongly in the concept of the bicultural nation, not only as an essential for the unity of Canada but as a sound social model, that it approaches a form of personal nationalism.[36] Thus for him protection of Canadian independence is important as a means for assuring continuance of the bicultural pattern as opposed to having it swallowed up in the U.S. melting-pot society.

It should not be understood from any of these comments that Trudeau is uncritical on the foreign investment issue. In the mid-1950s he wrote a good deal about the problem, one quotation from that era being regularly cited today: "Shall we suffer passively our situation of economic domination? . . . It would be better to be annexed outright by the United States than exploited without limit."[37] The point would seem to be rather that he has thought through a philosophy in which polarizing concepts like nationalism and dominance are replaced by functional and pragmatic guidelines as to the degrees of interdependence and independence which are useful for Canada and realistic in the modern world.

Trudeau, in accepting the fact of American dominance, concedes that Canada has only very limited control over its affairs. However, his concept of national identity is satisfied by the existence of a certain degree of decision-making autonomy within the Canadian government. His sort of federalist, functionalist thinking about the control structure of society would seem to be comfortable with the same general type of autonomy which, for example, the provinces have within the general Canadian government structure. Thus Canada could lose control over a still greater portion of actual economic and political matters in an absolute sense so long as it retained the political institutions and related power structure from which to assert control whenever it seemed desirable and practical to do so. All of this, of course, is conjectural and it is possible that recent events such as the U.S. DISC program may have changed Trudeau's attitudes by highlighting the vulnerability of Canada.

Other concepts of the degree of control necessary for national identity grade away from this in varied directions. So far as foreign investment is concerned, their main thrust is in the direction of formal and institutional aspects of industrial control. The extreme views consider that national identity requires that industrial decisions be entirely within Canadian hands, including both top executives in business and direct government control. The more moderate views are satisfied that national identity is protected if the industrial decision-making structure is responsive to national desires, which may be accomplished in a variety of ways that include regulatory measures, presence of Canadian nationals in management, or simply sensitivity of industrial executives to Canadian viewpoints.

Another approach looks more to the options open to Canadians in specific economic situations than to control of the whole economy. It accepts the fact that all nations, even the United States, are constrained in their overall economic control by international interdependence. The outlets for national identity therefore seem to lie in having sufficient control to realize fully the limited separate capabilities which each nation may have within it. This philosophy is concerned with preservation of enough elements of control in Canada so that the nation may exercise its identity when it so desires. Important objectives in pursuit of this philosophy are the support of Canadian entrepreneurs, the assurance that products appropriate to the distinctive life style of Canada can be developed, and the availability of opportunities for individuals to find employment within Canada according to their educational capabilities and personal inclinations.

It is in this context that the concept of the "truncated" firm emphasized in the Gray Report must be understood.[38] The truncated subsidiary is one in which key functions are absent, being in the hands of the parent organization. The deficiencies most often mentioned are top management, research and development, and exports. The question as defined by Carl Beigie, formerly executive director of the Private Planning Association of Canada, is whether "foreign-owned enterprises have become so predominant—reaching a certain 'critical mass'—that important gaps have emerged in Canada's capabilities."[39] If truncation is too great in too many industries, Canada does not have within its borders the capacity to pursue its own industrial initiatives. In the eyes of some people, that deficiency would mean the loss of national identity.

To round out this discussion of the meaning of national identity, it is appropriate to inject a summary of an article entitled

"Canada-U.S. Relations: Options for the Future," by External Affairs Minister Mitchell Sharp.[40] This article is generally understood in Canada to be a sequel to the series of earlier policy documents resulting from a broad review of Canadian foreign policy that set forth goals and guidelines for other aspects of Canada's international stance. While relations with the United States were mentioned in various places in these documents, there was no comprehensive treatment of that subject. In light of the overwhelming dominance of the United States in Canadian foreign policy, this gap had been criticized by many Canadians. Sharp's statement has filled the gap, providing as clear a definition as is likely to appear of the basic philosophy guiding government relations with the United States.

The document is also a good indicator of the central thrust of Canadian thinking, not only because of its official character but also because of the author. Mitchell Sharp is a long-time public servant who has demonstrated over many years a capacity to sense and represent the mood of the nation. Within the Liberal Party he has also been something of a bridge between the traditional philosophy of the group led by former Prime Minister Lester Pearson and the outlook of the newer group following Prime Minister Trudeau. His statement would seem to have these qualities, setting forth a guiding philosophy which is tuned into the main trends of current Canadian thinking and sufficiently balanced in adapting to them to achieve broad support. It is therefore a useful indicator of the prevailing attitudes.

While there are a number of specific points in Sharp's statement which will be mentioned in later sections, he concentrates on just a few central ideas. His main preoccupation is with "the continental pull" which has drawn Canada into greater ties with the United States, and will continue to do so. He observes that the consequent close interrelationship, "even as an inadvertent process, has acquired a momentum that, as one American student of Canadian affairs has recently put it, is 'subject to profound internal growth.'" The logics of proximity and similarity lead naturally to cultural and economic integration, and as the interaction proceeds, largely through the free action of private individuals and institutions, the ties between the nations become more numerous and stronger.

The central policy issue as stated by Sharp is: "What is to be done about the continental pull and the internal momentum with which it is thought by many to be endowed?" His analysis is guided by the dual criteria of distinctness and harmony. Accepting harmony with the United States as an obvious requisite, he focuses his main attention on distinctness. Three quotations convey the main thrust of his thought in defining the nature and utility of distinctness.

Distinctness has no autonomous virtue of its own. It is not an end in itself. In the process of nation-building, however, it is a substantial factor of cohesion. In the case of Canada, in particular, it is arguable that the perception of a distinct identity can make a real and discernible contribution to national unity. . . .

If Canadians say they want a distinct country, it is not because they think they are better than others. It is because they want to do the things they consider important and do them in their own way. And they want Canadian actions and life styles to reflect distinctly Canadian perspectives and a Canadian view of the world. . . .

In the broadest sense independence is related ultimately to the capacity of governments to formulate and conduct policy on the basis of national perceptions for the achievement of national objectives in the domestic and international environments. Distinctness, on the other hand, is an attribute that applies to a national society in all its various manifestations.

Basically, there are two goals here. One is the perceived desire of Canadians as a whole for distinctness which, on the basis of opinion polls and other information, Sharp observes has increased greatly in recent years. The second is the preservation of independent governmental capability, a line of thinking which is consistent with Trudeau's philosophy and Grant's concept of the government elite protecting the national superstructure, which will be discussed in the next section. Against these goals there is the practical constraint that only to a limited extent will Canadians forgo cultural and economic benefits to preserve distinctness.

The problem in 1972, as Sharp sees it, lies in a growing sense that "the underlying trend in the Canadian-U.S. relationship may be becoming less congenial to the conception of Canadian distinctness." He sets forth three policy options as possible responses to this situation. The first is that Canada go along as it has, reacting to problems as they arise, working out in each the best balance of results it can. He rejects this "reactive posture" as "not likely to represent much of an advance. On the contrary, if the continental pull is, in fact, becoming stronger, we may . . . have to run harder simply to stay in place."

The second option is to move deliberately toward closer integration with the United States. He accepts the value of such steps as the Automotive Trade Agreement and apparently opens the door to some further movement in that direction. But he feels that the loss of economic and quite possibly political distinctness if this approach is followed is a major deterrent. "In fact, it is a moot question whether this option, or any part of it, is politically tenable in the present or any foreseeable climate of Canadian public opinion."

"The third option would be, over time, to lessen the vulnerability of the Canadian economy to external factors, including, in particular, the impact of the United States and, in the process, to strengthen our capacity to advance basic Canadian goals and develop a more confident sense of national identity." This is the course Sharp prescribes as consistent with national goals and feasible. He stresses the "over time" aspect because the elements of national policy required (which will appear later in this study) can only evolve slowly, given cost and other constraints. The guiding philosophy, however, will be to build a Canada which is stronger and has more varied world relations, and thus is better able to maintain its distinctness.

Sharp's views are probably as close as one could come today to the central tendency of Canadian attitudes on the meaning of national identity and the basic ways to pursue it. But in light of the other views we have noted, the picture is not clear and that is probably the most important point to be observed about the whole subject. There is no consensus in Canada on the matter and there is unlikely to be one because of basic differences in personal psychology and in individual circumstances and goals, and because the feasibility of the options open to Canadians is so uncertain and is changing constantly. Thus the reality with which one must deal in assessing the situation is that a variety of viewpoints exist as to the extent and form of cultural, political, and economic identity which the country should seek to preserve as essential to the widely expressed desire for national identity.

The Spectrum of Attitudes

Of prime importance in the evolution of Canadian policy on foreign investment is the wide diversity of opinions. To get a feel for the spectrum of viewpoints, the population will be sliced in the following sections along several dimensions: regions, opinion groups, socioeconomic classes, and political parties.

REGIONAL DIFFERENCES

It is generally considered that Ontario is the center of adverse opinions toward foreign investment, with other regions taking more favorable views for varied reasons. The Maritime provinces and Quebec have severe unemployment problems and are extremely anxious for more investment, be it domestic or foreign. Furthermore, they have traditionally been dominated as much by Canadian firms based in Ontario as they have by foreign firms. The Prairie provinces in recent years have benefited greatly from an economic boom based on foreign investment, particularly the tremendous development of the petroleum resources in Alberta. And British Columbia, shut off behind the Rocky Mountains, has traditionally been oriented toward close integration with the U.S. Pacific states.

The survey results shown in Table 6 confirm this distribution in part and conflict with it in part. In both surveys the Quebec and Maritime responses were clearly more favorable to foreign firms than those from Ontario. Most striking, however, was the finding that the Western views were just as negative as those from respondents in Ontario. Apparently the good feeling engendered by the investment boom is now being replaced by negative reactions to major investments, notably the dominant position gained by the foreign companies which control most of the gas and petroleum firms on which the economy of the West is so dependent. An illustration of the type of situation which may be generating negative attitudes is the potash operation of a U.S. firm in Saskatchewan. During the recent recession, potash output had to be cut back. The company had operations in both Canada and the United States. It is generally believed in Canada, apparently with factual support, that the U.S. labor force was reduced less than that in Saskatchewan. However,

Table 6

Attitudes on Foreign Investment, Regional Distribution

**Question: Is U.S. ownership of Canadian companies a good or bad thing
for Canada?**

	Maritimes	Quebec	Ontario	Prairies	British Columbia
Bad thing	31%	41%	45%	48%	53%
Good thing	49%	42%	39%	33%	34%
Qualified or no opinion	20%	17%	16%	19%	12%

SOURCE: J. Alex Murray and Mary C. Gerace, "Canadian Attitudes toward the U.S. Presence," *Public Opinion Quarterly,* Fall 1972.

Question: Does Canada have enough U.S. capital?

	Maritimes	Quebec	Ontario	West
Enough	61%	58%	73%	69%
Need more	22%	31%	18%	19%
No opinion	17%	11%	9%	12%

SOURCE: Toronto *Daily Star,* February 12, 1972.

the differences in views among the various Western provinces are not as yet fully explained. We can only say that the data do confirm the continued presence of regional differences in viewpoints, which, we will note subsequently, is a significant factor in decision making on foreign investment.

OPINION GROUPS

While one can find in Canada all manner of shadings of opinions on foreign investment, it is useful to describe certain opinion groups. The hazards of oversimplification in this process are real but there is a substantial clustering of people around seven main patterns of thinking. One must also appreciate that the positions of these groups on specific policies have shifted, and probably will continue to, over time, and so my comments here define only where they tended to stand in 1973.

At one extreme of this spectrum are the *radical nationalists* who advocate a socialist reversal of the foreign investment

process. The organizational center for this approach is the
Waffle Group, and the most conspicuous leader is Professor
Melville Watkins of the University of Toronto. Watkins was
chairman of the task force which prepared the 1968 report on
foreign investment for the cabinet committee initially headed
by Walter Gordon (see Chapter 1). In a later book, Watkins
recorded his disgust with the failure of the committee to accept
the report and the unwillingness of the Liberal government to
act aggressively to check foreign investment.[41] He turned to the
New Democratic Party (NDP), and finding even its prevailing
philosophy too moderate, he joined with other people advocating a radical solution for the problem to form the Waffle Group.

The Wafflers are determined that Canadians should have full
control over their own economic affairs and that any significant
control of industry by foreign firms is inconsistent with this
goal. They do not believe that private enterprise in Canada is
capable of reasserting control over industry or that there is sufficient private capital to purchase back control of foreign-owned
subsidiaries. Thus, the only practical solution they see is nationalization of the foreign firms. Having started down the road of
socialism in this manner, the Wafflers tend to adopt related positions on labor and other questions.

While the NDP has essentially a democratic socialist philosophy, the extreme nationalism of the Waffle Group was not
acceptable to the majority of the NDP members. The conflict on
philosophical grounds was apparently augmented by personal
animosity on the part of many established NDP leaders, to
whom the aggressive tactics of the Wafflers were an organizational threat. There was constant controversy therefore within
the NDP from the time the Waffle Group took form at the party
convention in Edmonton in 1970. In mid-1972 the controversy
reached a climax. The Ontario NDP leadership gave the Wafflers
a choice of ceasing to function as a separate organizational unit
or leaving the party.

Faced with this ultimatum, the Ontario Wafflers convened a
conference in mid-August. The outcome was a split of the
group. Some 65 percent voted to set up a new group, Movement
for an Independent Socialist Canada (MISC), headed by Watkins and James Laxer, the chief Waffle leaders. They would
remain members of the NDP but carry on their active work out-

side it under the new banner. The balance of the group, led by Steven Penner, decided to remain in the NDP as a left-wing caucus. They were considered the more extreme socialists and communists. Their approach would be to work actively within the NDP against the policies of the party leadership but not to engage in the type of publicly visible activities to which the leadership had objected.

Numerically, the Waffle Group is a very small factor. It has a mailing list of only 2,500–3,000 people, according to Watkins.[42] Geographically it is limited in large part to Ontario and particularly Toronto. The membership is drawn largely from the intellectuals in academic and, to a much lesser degree, labor circles. Its strength lies in the aggressive, articulate qualities of its leadership, whose ideas are constant prods to the main body of national thinking. Undoubtedly their efforts have been a factor in moving Canadians as a whole toward stronger nationalistic attitudes on foreign investment, even though their particular solutions have only a very small following.

Moving back from the extreme end of the spectrum, we find a substantially larger group who may be labeled the *strong nationalists*. The philosophical center of this group is the Committee for an Independent Canada (CIC), organized in 1970 by Walter Gordon, the early pioneer of nationalistic reaction against foreign investment; Peter Newman, an outstanding newsman who was then editor of the Toronto *Daily Star,* the journalistic seat of Canadian nationalism, and is now editor of *Maclean's*; and Abraham Rotstein, professor of political economy at the University of Toronto. The CIC members share with the Waffle Group a determination to reassert Canadian control over the economy and a willingness to make sacrifices in the interest of Canadian independence. They differ from the Wafflers, however, in their intent to achieve their goals essentially within the established system of private enterprise and related governmental institutions.

In late 1972 the CIC commenced a process of major change in character and role. For its first two years it was guided by a general philosophy with little attempt at agreement on specific policy proposals. Its membership covered a very wide range of views running all the way from some who were close to the Waffle approach to others with a quite mild concept of how the foreign investment question should be handled. All political parties and walks of life were represented in the membership. The lack of a concrete program may or may not have been a deliberate strategy, but it would seem to have been an important factor in the breadth of CIC influence as measured, for example, by its obtaining 170,000 signatures on a petition to Trudeau in 1971. In this period the CIC seemed more of a national philosophical movement than a political action organization. It provided an emotional and intellectual meeting ground for a wide spectrum of people who shared a common concern for the future of Canadian national identity, even though they might differ substantially on what should be done about it. By virtue of the number of its adherents and the stature and dedication of the organizers, the CIC exerted a substantial, though nebulous, leadership in the upsurge of nationalistic reaction to foreign investment.

In September 1972, the CIC held a policy conference in Edmonton, the outcome of which changes its image and will probably alter its membership. The delegates voted on some 202 specific policy proposals concerning foreign ownership, Canadian capital, trade unions, energy and the north, land, education, cinema and television, and the arts.[43] With a few exceptions the proposals were overwhelmingly supported, i.e., "yes" votes of seventy or more with "no" votes of ten or fewer. Thus, instead of the former vague philosophical image, the CIC now has a very concrete and broad specific program.

Despite its many details the program has a central character which can be defined fairly concisely. The goal of reasserting Canadian control over the society would be pursued by a wide range of specific measures—tax changes, investment controls, subsidies, land ownership regulations, and the like. *In toto* these measures would add up to a very substantial increase of social direction of national affairs, largely by the government. For example, nationalization would take place by cooperative direction of government and industry councils; all foreign investments would be screened, with the review covering all significant activities; "the government should ask and, if necessary, require the chartered banks to devote more of their vast resources to higher risk enterprises"; and unions would be detached from U.S. affiliation by several steps such as requiring small sections of internationals to merge with larger units.

The CIC continues to differ from the Wafflers in rejecting outright socialism. But their program is similar to the Wafflers' in philosophically accepting the assumption that the goals desired cannot be achieved without strong assertion of social intent through government intervention in the economy. Thus in effect the CIC brand of nationalism requires acceptance of a cost in social freedom along with whatever economic costs may be involved in establishing the degree of economic independence sought.

The character of the CIC approach as it has now emerged may be expected to have a pronounced effect on its membership. Rather than attracting people with a wide range of views who share a common general concern with the problem of Canadian independence, its members will now presumably be largely those who agree with the program and underlying philosophy adopted at Edmonton. One might expect these members to find it a more satisfactory organization in which their energies can be directed strongly to clear action goals. On the other hand, there will be a certain portion of those who were attracted to the ideals of the CIC in the early period who will find unacceptable the social costs of CIC's concept of achieving its goals. The presumption then would be that numerically the CIC would have fewer adherents but that the vigor of their support would be greater henceforth. The magnitude of its membership will be a good indication of the trend of nationalistic feelings in Canada for, to borrow Walter Gordon's phrase, the CIC program does provide a realistic "choice for Canada."[44] That is, compared to the Waffler socialism, which is so far from Canadian reality that it is not conceivable, the CIC program could fit in Canadian life if the nationalistic desires were strong enough to accept its costs.

The third group may be called the *moderate nationalists* to distinguish them from the strong nationalists identified with the CIC. The moderate nationalists do not generally speak in terms of a set of positive actions to reverse the foreign investment process or of national sacrifices to achieve this goal. Rather, they advocate efforts to move toward more independence of Canadian industry by encouragement to Canadian firms, and making foreign firms serve the national interest better while protecting the Canadian standard of living. They conceive of this approach as a form of "positive nationalism" which builds the national sector without significantly obstructing the foreign-owned portion. There is no organization representing this viewpoint, but it appears to be the dominant attitude among the majority of Canadians in and out of government.

In reality, the appearance that this approach does not involve sacrifice by Canadians is not valid. The difference between it and the approach of the strong nationalists is simply that the cost of the latter is greater and more visible. The measures advocated by the moderate nationalists, such as subsidies, differential tax advantages, etc., to support Canadian firms have a cost to the standard of living, but it is somewhat more hidden and smaller than policies which could result in direct reduction of new foreign investment. In sum, therefore, we may characterize the moderate nationalists as advocating policies which reduce the role of foreign firms gradually by building up national firms through actions which carry only small costs to the people, sufficiently hidden so they are scarcely felt.

The next three groups should be discussed together because, while their underlying attitudes are different, there is considerable similarity in their positions on foreign investment. The three may be labelled as the *internationalists,* the *nonnationalists* and the *unconcerned.* Distinguishing between the first two at times seems like philosophical gobbledygook. But there is substance to it. The internationalist is a nationalist. He has feelings about Canada, wants it to be strong among nations, and so forth. But he believes in the maximum development of internationalization of economic and political structuring as a means to provide for the security and economic welfare of his own people and others. With this orientation he is essentially favorable to the concept of the multinational firm as an internationally optimizing economic institution. His response to the problems it creates runs most naturally in the direction of international control. At the Canadian national level he may endorse measures to compensate for the present lack of effective international control, but their logics must be consistent in his mind with the international efficiency outlook, not strictly Canadian nationalistic goals.

The nonnationalist, on the other hand, has made a philosophical break with nationalism. One suspects that at some level (e.g., hockey or respect for the flag) he will show some nascent nationalism. But on major economic issues the nonnationalist does not consider such criteria as making Canada strong among nations. Canada is no more critical as an entity to him than his city or province. He therefore is basically opposed to nationalistically directed goals as contrary to the concept of a nonnationalist world.

The unconcerned are those who are apathetic and attitudinally uninvolved in these matters. One might describe them as anationalistic as distinguished from the nonnationalists for whom the *non* element is of some philosophical importance. The unconcerned are either not appreciably conscious of the whole idea of nationalism or have no position on it one way or the other. Typically they are people to whom the main focus of life is family-job-social group and broader things do not matter. Again, as with the nonnationalists, one suspects that there is some nascent nationalism in these people, that when the Canadian hockey team beat the Russians something stirred in their hearts. But on economic questions their lack of concern with nationalism is real.

So far as foreign investment policy is concerned, all of the people in these three categories tend to come out in pretty much the same place. They will opt for a laissez-faire economic stance. They are distinguished from the moderate nationalists in that they will not support the cost and complications of the special efforts to subsidize, push or favor Canadian firms to build them up vis-à-vis foreign-owned ones. That is, they believe in a truly open, nondiscriminatory economy in which the role of foreign firms evolves according to market forces without special nationalistically oriented influences. Some, notably among the internationalists, do favor a degree of special handling of multinational firms, in marginal areas like extraterritorial application of foreign laws. But these are minor departures from the main thrust of their thinking.

Trying to fit any specific individual into one of these three categories is difficult and not worth the effort since, for practical purposes, their views are similar. However, without trying to classify him, I will for illustrative purposes cite the position of one person to give substance to the generalization. W. Earle McLaughlin, chairman of the Royal Bank of Canada, would fit among the internationalists or nonnationalists. In a *Reader's Digest* article he sets forth his philosophy. Two quotes give its flavor: "In general, I favor an open-door policy on foreign ownership." "If our economic objectives are a higher rate of growth, greater price stability, a better standard of living, they would be better accomplished by freer trade with all countries and our first step should be to urge and support measures for freer multinational trade."[45]

We have now arrived at the other end of the spectrum held by the *continentalists,* a term long established in the Canadian vocabulary to describe those who essentially believe in union of Canada and the United States. While in the early days continentalism was often associated with political union, the advocates of full integration are very rare today. The majority of those described as continentalists essentially are advocates of a high degree of economic integration. Specifically, they favor a common market with a free flow of trade and investment between Canada and the United States and integrated handling of such matters as energy. Explicit advocates of continentalism are not organized like the CIC, so they are harder to identify and count. Nonetheless, they would appear to be probably as numerous and influential as the CIC. Just as one indication, we may note that the concept of the common market with the United States has been advocated at a premiers' conference in 1971 by the then Premier of British Columbia, W. A. C. Bennett, and was endorsed by Premier Campbell of Prince Edward Island. Subsequently, Andre Raynauld, chairman of the Economic Council of Canada, said he was "not very far" from Bennett in the degree of freedom of trade he felt desirable.[46] It should be observed that all continentalists do not believe integration with the United States is necessarily good. Many simply regard it as inevitable and feel it is best to accept that fact and make the best of it.

As a visible political program, continentalism is necessarily a limited factor, particularly in the current Canadian mood. A true continentalist is by definition an antinationalist, and that is a position of which society in general does not approve. As Peter Dobell observes in his book, to many Canadians "continentalism is treason."[47] Only a few Canadians therefore speak out clearly like Senator Grosart: "I believe that integration, on a planned and programmed basis, of our economy with that of the United States is absolutely necessary."[48] Most people with leanings in this direction limit themselves to advocating specific integration moves, notably a free trade area concept, while adhering to nationalistically acceptable positions on political, cultural, and other matters. Still, in the popular literature of Canada these people are generally castigated as continentalists and are viewed by those in the other groups as advocating measures which will weaken Canadian nationhood. Thus in the visible give-and-take of political processes, their influence is less than that of the nationalists of varying colors who are able to appeal to more popular emotional responses. The continentalists' influence accordingly is exerted rather in the less visible processes of government decision making, reinforced by basic economic arguments which will be considered in subsequent sections. The future of their influence lies essentially in the strength of these economic considerations.

SOCIOECONOMIC CLASSES

Looking at the Canadian population along its socioeconomic dimensions, we find some distinct differences in attitudes. A basic statistical framework for comparisons here is provided by my surveys described above, to which illustrative evidence is added from a variety of published sources.

The data given in Table 3 (p. 18) indicate that there is some differentiation according to social groups within the general public; those with an academic orientation or lower on the income scale tend toward more negative views, while the responses become more favorable as one progresses up the economic scale. However, the diversity of responses lying behind the averages reported in the data demonstrates the wide range of views. The in-depth study of attitudes in a Canadian city reported in Perry's *Galt, U.S.A.* provides a vivid picture of the reasons for these differences in views, many of them closely associated with the personal experiences and satisfactions which individuals have encountered in their relations with foreign firms.[49] Other data in my questionnaire showed a strong correlation between the attitude toward foreign firms and the degree of satisfaction in personal contacts with the firms.

Somewhat fuller conclusions can be reached about the attitudes in the key elite decision-making groups of the nation. It is readily evident from the survey data and numerous public utterances that, while some individual businessmen have a CIC-nationalistic orientation, the business community as a whole tends to be relatively favorable to foreign investment. Business-men are pragmatic in nature, and by and large their experi-ence with the economy dominated by foreign enterprise has been quite satisfactory. The adverse experiences seem to be most often directly related to competitive situations in which foreign firms are hurting the interests of Canadian companies. A good example of this was apparently provided in the debate in 1971 over the control of investment firms in Ontario. While a case was made to the effect that Canadian development would be best protected if ownership of investment firms were limited to Canadians, a number of Canadian observers claimed that the main impetus for the efforts to resist foreign ownership came from Toronto investment houses seeking to protect their per-sonal interests against strong competition from more aggres-sive and better-financed foreign firms.[50]

An interesting parallel is found in the study of the magazine industry by the Davey Committee of Parliament, published in 1970.[51] An earlier study of the industry had reported a general adverse opinion of foreign publications by Canadian magazine publishers. This position apparently was based on their feeling that U.S. magazines were depriving them of too large a portion of the Canadian advertising dollar. By 1971, however, the majority of publishers had swung over to acceptance of the prevailing situation in which *Time* and the *Reader's Digest* dom-inated the field, with a number of small Canadian publications dividing up the balance of the advertising income. Their stated logic was that the two major publications supported the overall magazine advertising field in competition with other media, particularly television. Only a small number of publications which competed directly with the U.S. magazines expressed an adverse view. It would appear from these facts that what had happened was that the industry had shaken out over the period between the two studies, and the majority of participants in it were now those to whom the existing structure was essentially satisfactory.

Extending this logic broadly, one can readily observe that if the economy and industry were progressing overall in a reasonably satisfactory manner, the majority of participants in it, including both Canadian business firms and Canadian managers in the foreign-owned firms, would essentially be satisfied with the structure as it was. By and large therefore, the business community in Canada is a strong supporter of the status quo on foreign investments. Such nationalism as most businessmen may have seems likely to express itself in support of cultural identity and minor moves to increase Canadian political and economic control which will not appreciably upset the economic applecart. Otherwise, their active efforts may be expected, as in the case of the Ontario investment house situation, to be limited to specific competitive situations.

The opinions of the two government groups in Table 3 are a little more adverse toward foreign companies than those of the business leaders. These data conform to a logical expectation that the government leaders would be more concerned with the difficulties of exercising control over the affairs of the country because of foreign ownership of business. They also fit with conceptual views such as those of George Grant, who observes that the civil service is the essential element by which nationhood is preserved.[52] Nonetheless, the government leaders are generally favorable in their appraisal, the critical judgments falling primarily in the control questions. In part, these moderate views may be attributable to the fact that for every situation in which there is an adverse effect from the presence of foreign companies for the responsibilities of a government leader, there is likely to be another situation in which the presence of the multinational firms makes an important positive contribution.

A breakdown of the responses according to government ministries did not indicate any significant differences which could be related to the effects of multinational firms in particular aspects of national affairs. It would appear from this evidence that varied attitudes are quite randomly distributed through the bureaucracy. In personal interviewing one gains the impression that those with more negative views are likely to be those in positions where complications due to the multinational firms have been experienced most significantly, but that the personal inclinations of individuals will be quite as important as the immediate practical experience.

Grant makes another observation which may be quite perceptive as to the evolution of attitudes among bureaucrats. He says
that many of them feel that they are part of an international
bureaucracy and therefore are not as concerned about the complications in the management of national affairs as might be
expected.[53] It may be premature to think in these terms with
respect to the middle range of government civil servants, but
it is certainly true that the higher one goes the more they tend
to be negotiating frequently with Washington and other foreign
government organizations. The dimensions of this role are suggested by the fact that there were 12,900 official Canadian visits
to Washington in 1968.[54] These interactions contribute a different set of satisfactions from those acquired from simply man-
aging affairs within one nation's borders. The psychology here
would seem to be closely related to that which has already been
described in the makeup of Prime Minister Trudeau. This may
be a factor contributing to the greater favorability toward foreign business found among top officials when my elite survey
data were broken down according to levels in the government
hierarchy. Former cabinet minister Eric Kierans has caustically
referred to this psychology among bureaucrats who keep close
social contact with multinational business executives, which is
offensive to nationalistic concepts of preserving Canadian identity.[55] Nonetheless, looking to the future, one may see the possibility that an increase in the number and effectiveness of
international governmental institutions offering greater opportunities for this sort of satisfaction will provide a strong offsetting influence to compensate for the losses in immediate
control of national affairs which growing interdependence
involving multinational firms will cause for government officials.

The labor leaders in the elite survey expressed a distinctly
more adverse view of foreign companies than the other three
groups. This difference was noted also in my surveys in Britain
and France, and it seems quite likely that it is due in substantial
part to ideological views about big business in general rather
than to any particular bias against foreign firms.[56] There were
three questions in the survey which asked the respondents to
compare the treatment by foreign companies with that by local
national firms with respect to wages, other working conditions,
and relations with unions. On all three questions the Canadian

labor leaders were essentially in agreement with the other elites in attributing somewhat more favorable performance to the foreign companies than the local ones. It is particularly interesting to note that on the question of relations of trade unions with foreign companies, the union leaders were clearly favorable to the foreign firms, as contrasted to rather negative views expressed by both British and French labor leaders. In view of the large amount of experience of the unions with foreign firms, this must be taken as a well-considered judgment. Presumably, it has much to do with the fact that proximity to the United States has resulted in substantial benefit both in the practices of the firms themselves and in close association with the strength of U.S. union groups.

Nonetheless, the clearly more negative views from the labor leaders are a source of concern to the extent that they represent a large and powerful body of public opinion. While the responses from the lower income groups in the general public study noted in Table 3 were rather slim, they are still useful as an indication that the labor leaders' views are more or less representative of their membership in this relatively negative appraisal.* These attitudes appear in policy statements by union officials. The Canadian Labour Congress criticized the Foreign Takeovers Review bill as too weak, calling for screening of all new investments and supervision of behavior of multinational firms.[57] The Ontario unions have presented a brief to the provincial government that advocates strong action on multinational firms, including assurance of more jobs for Canadians in nationalization plans.

However, the main body of labor leaders is clearly not extremist in its views. The Waffle Group made a strong effort to steer auto union groups into support of its positions in 1971–1972 and was firmly rejected. Likewise, in my interviews, Canadians generally concurred that despite negative public statements about foreign investment, labor leaders took a rather pragmatic, essentially favorable view of foreign firms. Their overriding concern was for more jobs, and second to that was improved working conditions, both matters on which the

---

*Not all union members are low income, of course. But the weighting of labor groups is in that direction.

foreign-controlled firms were viewed favorably. Their negative opinions were related more to specific actions like plant shutdowns than a general desire to check foreign investment.

There is, however, some emerging sense of concern as an outgrowth of the Nixon actions of August 15, 1971, DISC, and U.S. labor protectionism, including its support of the Burke-Hartke bill. What labor leaders fear is that Canadian jobs in multinational firms may be eroded by decisions based on political pressures by U.S. labor that are outside their control. This concern does not lead directly to an anti-foreign-investment posture. Indeed, to the contrary, it directs labor to actions designed to check the possible exodus of foreign operations.

The only clear direction of strong action is a growing tension between Canadian unions and U.S. "internationals," with whom many of them are affiliated. Officials of the Canadian Labour Congress have made strong statements protesting the advocacy of the Burke-Hartke bill by the AFL-CIO. The CLC is particularly annoyed because it appears that the payments its unions make to the U.S. internationals are being used to lobby for legislation which will hurt Canadian workers. This specific issue is part of a broader question of the degree of control exercised by the U.S. international unions over Canadian affiliates. That question contributes to the nationalistic attitudes in Canada, but it is not directly part of the foreign investment issue and therefore it is not discussed here.

POLITICAL PARTIES

The positions of the leading political parties on foreign investment can be discussed at two levels. Superficially and for many practical purposes, the story is very simple. The Conservatives and Liberals have similar moderate nationalist views and the New Democratic Party is strongly nationalistic. But the Conservatives and Liberals do have somewhat different positions, and these differences will be significant for the future, especially in light of the uncertain political prospects coming out of the 1972 election. It should be emphasized that this discussion concerns party "positions" and not the views of individual party members, which, in the major parties, cover a very wide span as the elaboration later in this section will demonstrate.

Considering first the major characteristics, we can readily

observe the general tenor of the party views. My survey of elites, described earlier, provided a breakdown of opinions of members of Parliament by party. The overall appraisal of the effects of foreign firms on Canada (question 1 in Table 3) showed average scores as follows: Liberals, 2.7; Conservatives, 2.8; and NDP, 5.3 (Good=1, Bad=7). On other questions the same general pattern was repeated, the members of the two major parties running in a narrow range and the NDP members consistently more adverse in their views.

A broad look at the positions taken by the parties or their key spokesmen on major foreign investment issues confirms this basic pattern. Appendix 3 presents a comprehensive analysis of positions. A brief summary of that information suffices to place the parties in the spectrum of opinions.

Inflow of new foreign investment. Neither the Conservatives nor the Liberals have proposed any serious obstacles to continued new foreign capital input. The NDP has clearly said that it should be discouraged, though only mild measures have been suggested, such as lowering the interest rate to discourage foreign capital.

Buying back foreign investment. The two major parties have disclaimed this goal as unwise and impractical. The NDP has supported the idea in general and has advocated some specific steps, such as use of $5 billion of currently held foreign exchange reserves to buy stock in major foreign-owned firms.

Screening. The Liberal government proposed the review system for takeovers, and the Conservatives supported it with minor modifications. Moderate expansion of screening to some new investments was proposed by the Liberals in 1973. Rigorous screening of all sorts of new foreign investments is a major NDP objective. The NDP also visualizes the screening process as quite severely restrictive as compared to the rather open approach, with the emphasis directed at maximizing benefits, not excluding investments, contemplated by the other parties.

Key sectors. The Conservatives give much more emphasis than the Liberals in their policy statements to measures to protect Canadian interests in key sectors. However, the Liberal government enacted much of the key sector legislation in the 1960s, and the difference between the two parties on this issue is seemingly not great. The NDP does not stress key sectors but apparently would go at least as far as the others in this respect.

Building up Canadian firms vs. foreign-owned firms. There are three broad aspects to this subject:

Financial grants. The NDP would stop all grants for research, new plants in depressed areas, etc., for foreign firms. The Conservatives and Liberals would move in this direction but only in a mild way.

Incentives for investment in Canadian firms. All of the parties advocate tax incentives and other measures for this purpose, with no clear difference among their positions.

Financing for Canadian firms. The Canada Development Corporation was pushed by the Liberals for several years and was set up by their government. The Conservatives have consistently opposed the CDC, preferring changes in the Industrial Development Bank as a means to improve financing. The NDP was a strong advocate of the CDC but it has bitterly opposed the form it has taken; its philosophy calls for government ownership and a more positive approach to using the capital to build up Canadian vs. foreign firms.

Boards of directors. The Conservatives have endorsed the requirement of a majority of Canadians on corporate boards as a key element in their foreign investment policy. The Liberals have played this idea down as of minor value but have included it in their 1973 legislative program, apparently as a concession to the Conservatives. The NDP would appear to agree with the Liberal view, saying that control of management decisions must be exerted directly by the Canadian government.

Financial disclosure. The Conservatives stress the requirement of greater financial reporting by foreign-owned firms. The Liberals do not speak out on this point but, since their government has put through certain reporting requirements, presumably it is of somewhat similar importance in their eyes. The NDP has supported financial disclosure but has not pushed this point recently, apparently regarding it as less important than other goals.

The overall pattern here is readily summarized. Both the Conservatives and the Liberals advocate quite moderate efforts to assure that foreign investment serves Canadian interests and to build up Canadian firms relative to the foreign-owned segment. The NDP, on the other hand, favors a strong approach to reducing and controlling the role of foreign investment. Its program is similar to that of the Committee for an Independent Canada but not so extreme as that of the Wafflers, with whom the main body of NDP members were never in agreement.

Grouping the two major parties together as moderate nationalists indicates the general direction in which they will guide foreign investment policy. But it leaves unanswered the question of how the parties differ in their approaches, a question of considerable interest when there is a good chance that government control may switch from one to the other over the next few years. I devoted a substantial research effort to exploring differences in visible party positions to try to determine their implications for the future. The results, summarized in Appendix 3, provide some interesting insights but they are far from conclusive.

As background for this discussion, it is well to present a brief picture of the character of the main parties, even though their characteristics are by no means well defined. Both are essentially coalitions of mixed social, economic, ethnic, and geographic dimensions. As a consequence there is not much differentiation in their basic thrust. As John Porter observes:

> The most significant characteristic of the two parties . . . is the fact that they share the same conservative values. Both have at times been responsible for reform legislation which might suggest progressive values, but their steps to the left have been taken more with a spirit of opportunism than from a basic orientation to social progress and change. . . . It is not that Canadian social structure is so static that it has no immanent potential for dynamic politics; it is rather that Canada's basically opportunistic parties have not harnessed this potential in the political system. They have either ignored these basic social differences or covered them up in the pretence that they do not exist.[58]

Porter's book, published in 1965, is adequate in its focus on the Canadian political system dominated by the two main parties. To complete the picture, the role of the New Democratic Party, founded in 1961, must be injected. As compared to the basic conservatism of the major parties, it has provided the element of dynamic, progressive politics which Porter found lacking in the earlier history. It has taken the lead in pushing for various forms of social legislation, much of which was subsequently adopted by the Liberal Party. It has performed a similar role in the foreign investment field, taking the initiative in advocating stronger measures which have in time been picked up by the Liberals.

Returning to the two main parties, one finds upon digging deeper that despite the overall common conservative, opportunist thrust, there are some moderate differences in the parties that are relevant. A study of the 1968 federal election by John Meisel showed that there was a little differentiation in the characteristics of supporters of the two parties.[59] The Conservatives apparently appealed slightly more to those in the lower middle classes, with the Liberals receiving a higher portion of the upper class votes. It was also found from attitude studies of voters that the proportion of Conservative support "increased with increases in the authoritarianism, law and order and cynicism scores and decreased with the respondents' higher moral liberalism, greater toleration of minorities, increased interest in foreign affairs, centralism with respect to Canadian Federalism, higher interest in the election, greater sense of efficacy and heightened optimism about the future generally and about one's economic prospects in particular."[60]

A point of caution must be injected about these findings. In 1968 the Liberals had a much greater edge over the Conservatives—46 percent vs. 31 percent—than in 1972, when the popular vote margin was 39 percent to 35 percent. The differences in voter characteristics derived from the study quoted above were based on statistical differences of fairly small magnitude. For example, 39 percent of Liberal voters were lower class as compared to 45 percent of Conservative voters. It is quite possible that the characteristics of the switch voters would change or eliminate the apparent differences in some characteristics if a similar study were made of 1972 voters. In other words, the study compares the hard-core Conservatives with the hard-core Liberals plus the switch voters, and changing the latter to the other side might convey a different picture. In any case, the characteristics are based on relatively small statistical differences, so they should not be taken as describing strong party differentiation. One may only say that there is an indication that the Conservatives are based somewhat more on lower economic groups and people with somewhat more traditionalist, conservative leanings.

These general characterizations must also be modified on a regional basis. For example, the survey indicated that in their areas of greatest strength, the Maritimes and Ontario, the Conservatives attracted above-average support from upper class people. This point is important in emphasizing the fallacies of simple characterizations. But it is more significant in discussing party positions. It is the elected party members who wield the greatest strength in federal and provincial party councils. Thus, for example, the fact that MPs from Ontario and the Maritimes, who account for the major portion of the Conservative caucus, were predominantly elected by a higher portion of upper and middle class people than in Canada as a whole tells us more about the way the party position will lean than the gross national data heavily weighted by lower class Quebecans who elected only two Conservative MPs in 1972. As a practical matter it is generally considered that the Conservatives in the House of Commons do represent a somewhat more conservative orientation than the Liberals, based on a combination of lower-middle-class traditionalism, particularly of a Prairie-Diefenbaker style, and some strong big-business influence. The Liberals seem somewhat more open to change, with a greater constituency among professionals and progressive businessmen. But, again, it must be stressed that the differences are of small magnitude.

Striking off in another direction, one finds that historically the images of the parties differ on relations with the United States. Dennis Smith notes:

The Conservative Party represents and contains the latent anti-Americanism which has been the precondition of the country's existence since 1867. Without always exposing this feeling in its crudity, the party has come to power in 1911, 1930, and 1957 on surges of anti-American emotion and when in office has been prepared to contemplate legislative restrictions on American economic and cultural influence in Canada, if such restrictions promise political advantage. When the anti-American devil slumbers in Canadian breasts, the Conservative party loses some of its sense of purpose. The national Liberal party, in contrast, has represented the opposite desire of Canadians: to conciliate the United States, to avoid antagonizing the giant, to enter into a North American partnership.[61]

To keep this quotation in proper perspective, it should be considered together with the emphasis on opportunism in the earlier quote. While there may be some greater degree of basic anti-Americanism among Conservatives, it appears also that anti-Americanism has turned out to be one of their opportunistic roles. As a party which has been out more than in (twenty-one years in power vs. fifty-one for the Liberals since 1900), it has capitalized on the limited periods of negative emphasis in Canada–United States relations, as compared to the Liberals who have administered the main flow of the relationship, which is historically dominated by an amicable, conciliatory approach.

A final background element which should be noted for future reference is the relation of provincial and federal party organizations. While there are varying degrees of cooperation between the two levels, the extent of separation of organizations and differences in viewpoints is a notable feature of Canadian politics compared to the relative closeness of most state and national party structures in the United States. This characteristic is most strikingly observed in the minor party situation in the Prairies. Manitoba and Saskatchewan are both controlled at the provincial level by the NDP, yet in the 1972 national elections the NDP took only seven of the twenty-six seats in those provinces. At the substantive level, the NDP provincial leaders have clearly disassociated themselves from the federal positions of NDP leader David Lewis. For example, Premier Schreyer of Manitoba asserted: "We are not socialists; do not believe the nonsense the Lewises are feeding the people of Canada. We are free enterprisers."[62]

Among the major parties the provincial-federal rapport seems to be better. For example, Conservative Premier Davis of Ontario worked hard for Robert Stanfield, his party's national leader, in the 1972 election. Still, it is recognized that the provincial party organizations are essentially autonomous and that the positions a party adopts at one level are not necessarily similar to those at the other. In the present discussion this point is particularly relevant in considering such questions as the degree to which the policies on foreign investment adopted by the Ontario Conservative government might be indicative of what a federal Conservative government might do. The answer is that the traditional patterns of provincial-federal party relations do not provide any real indication. The adoption of Ontario ideas at the federal level would depend upon assorted forces in the federal party system—personalities, economic pressures, regional differences, etc.—of which views from Ontario would be but one.

With this background in mind, we may look at the specific issues on which the Conservatives and Liberals have visibly differed. The Foreign Takeovers Review bill proposed in 1972 provided the only recent clear opportunity for direct confrontation between the two parties on a general foreign investment policy issue. The outcome was informative if not definitive.

The official Liberal position was manifest in the decision to present the bill. That there was substantial disagreement within the party was also readily observed. Ian Wahn, along with some thirteen other Liberal MPs, endorsed the stand of the Committee for an Independent Canada that the bill was entirely inadequate. Robert Kaplan, chairman of the Commons committee which reviewed the bill, spoke publicly outside of Parliament in favor of the screening of all investments recommended by the Gray Report.[63] While there were no Liberals who spoke strongly against the bill as going too far, it seems likely that there were some who inclined to that side of the issue.

The Conservative view was not so clearly defined. The logical place to look for a definition of its official position is the opposition speech in Commons immediately after the opening government argument. Gordon Fairweather's comments in this role convey the impression that the Conservatives accepted the principle of the review system, but the speech was notably vague in grappling with the issues. The most specific statement was: "I feel Bill C-201 in no way goes to the root of the problems created by direct foreign investment in Canada. This is not to say it is not a partial solution."[64] Beyond this he dealt in very general terms with the constitutionality of the bill, the need for a general industrial strategy and guidelines for review, and the merits of other approaches to foreign investments, such as key sector expansion and international control. The consensus among people I interviewed in Ottawa seemed to be that the speech was indicative of the wide division of views within the party. The assumption was that the party caucus had failed to agree on a clear policy on the bill, so Fairweather had been instructed to say as little as he respectably could.

This division of views was clear in other phases of the Commons debate. Fairweather personally has participated in CIC conferences, and even though as a Maritime MP he values the job creation role of foreign investment, he would evidently like to see a stronger approach to the foreign investment issue. On the other hand, as a spokesman for the party he presented the amendment in the committee hearings on the bill to change the criterion for approval of takeovers from their being "of significant benefit to Canada" to "being not detrimental to the national interests of Canada."[65] The viewpoint pushing in that more moderate direction was most evident in the hammering criticism of the bill in the hearings by Marcel Lambert, the Conservative financial expert. It was quite clear that he was basically opposed to the bill though, for practical purposes, he limited his efforts to trying to moderate its effects by proposing numerous specific changes.

Another good indicator of the Conservative position was the first reaction of party leader Stanfield when the bill was presented to Commons. His comments in their order of presentation were: that the bill contained no positive effort to increase Canadian ownership of industry; that the lack of procedure for provincial consultation was a serious weakness; that screening was acceptable in principle but sound guidelines were needed; and that greater financial disclosure by foreign firms and Canadian representation on boards of directors should be required.[66] One more significant item was the opinion expressed by Premier Davis of Ontario that the takeover review system was inadequate and stronger measures should be taken.

Overall, the indications are that the Conservatives accepted the takeover bill but that the moderating influences in their ranks were stronger than those among the Liberals, so that a somewhat milder approach was advocated.

The only other recent issue related to foreign investment upon which there has been a clear opportunity for legislative confrontation was the act establishing the Canada Development Corporation that passed in early 1971. The Liberals had been advocating the CDC since 1963. The time required to achieve it is not excessive in the legislative history of nonpressure progress of new institutions. But it is an indication of the absence of a strong favorable consensus in the party. The Conservatives had given relatively little attention to the idea during this period. A party subgroup preparing policy proposals in 1967 rejected the CDC concept in favor of improved efficiency of the private capital market and better utilization of the Industrial Development Bank.[67] Another subgroup endorsed expansion of the IDB in 1969 with no reference to the CDC.[68]

When the CDC bill was presented in 1971, the Liberals stated that it had two purposes: to help develop Canadian-controlled corporations and to give Canadians greater opportunities to invest in economic development in Canada. The Conservative opposition centered on a question put by their leader, Robert Stanfield: "Will the CDC . . . be anything more than a publicly sponsored private investment company working along traditional lines in the interest of people who hold shares in it?"[69] Since the CDC would be responsible to private owners and charged with earning a profit, it would essentially compete with existing capital sources. Any projects it could finance within its profit-making obligation presumably could obtain capital without government help. There was no prospect, therefore, that the CDC would serve national interests in any special way; it would simply draw investment capital to itself, away from other sectors of the capital market.

It would appear that the division between the parties on this issue is chiefly one of basic economic philosophy. Both have in general favored building up Canadian-owned firms, and greater availability of capital is accepted as a useful policy. However, the CDC to some degree competes with or replaces private financial institutions in undertaking equity participation in new ventures. The IDB is less a factor in this regard because it concentrates on debt capital. In any case, it was already in existence, so those with a conservative bent, feeling a pressure to support some effort to provide more capital, would tend to favor it in preference to the new institution.

Two other issues may best be discussed together. In their recent declarations the Conservatives have stressed Canadianization of boards of directors and greater financial disclosure. The Liberals have played down the former and indicated no interest in pushing the latter. The substance of these issues will be discussed in Chapter 5. It will suffice at this point to observe that the board-of-directors and disclosure proposals are apparently rather minor in that they would neither have much effect on performance of foreign firms nor cause them much complication.

There are two lines of reasoning which might explain the Conservative emphasis on these points. One is that they represent directions in which one can move at least a little to improve the performance of foreign-owned firms while still not interfering with the basic freedom of management decision making, as compared, for example, to the direct intervention in the screening process. This logic would be consistent with the Conservative philosophy evident in the position on the CDC.

The other rationale is that the position is strictly opportunistic. The Conservatives are under pressure to offer something different to counter the initiative gained by the Liberals in the public eye by pressing the screening approach. The board-of-directors and disclosure measures, while minor in actual impact, have some distinguishing features which are appealing. They apply to all foreign firms, not just the marginal group affected by limited screening. They appear to influence a much broader range of operational matters on a continuing basis. Thus the Conservatives can make a fair case that these steps are in fact a stronger effort to deal with foreign investment than the degree of screening proposed by the Liberals. The Conservative position is therefore probably based on a combination of the conservative desire to avoid direct interference with management and the opportunistic desire to have a differentiated position.

The final issue on which an appearance of difference is given is the stress on the key sector approach by the Conservatives. The problem in discussing this is that the Conservatives have never been specific about what industries they would extend the approach to or about the other forms of expansion their position might imply. Meantime the Liberals have consistently endorsed the concept, and in small ways they have extended it recently, for example, in proposing new support for book publishing in 1972. One has a strong impression, therefore, that there is no real difference here. The constant Conservative stress on the general issue without implementing details would appear to be most significant as an indication of the limited degree of real differentiation between the parties but of the strong desire to give the appearance of a degree of differentiation in order to appeal to the public.

Another perspective on the differences between the major parties is provided by the 1972 election campaign. In the main, foreign investment policy was conspicuous by its negligible role in campaign debates. In a policy paper dealing with Canada–United States economic relations issued four weeks before the election, the Conservatives noted briefly that the presence of many multinational firms "retarded Canada's ability to make its own decisions" in some instances. About ten days before the election they issued two more policy papers bearing on foreign investment. One proposed a major tax credit for income from investment in small firms designed to foster Canadian-owned businesses. The other set forth main points of Conservative policy on foreign investment following a familiar pattern: consultation with the provinces on policy, effective guidelines for behavior of foreign firms, financial disclosure, Canadianization of boards of directors, protection from extraterritorial application of foreign laws, and development of the key sector approach. This statement evoked no Liberal response, and the Conservatives made no effort to press it other than in one speech by Stanfield. Thus the issue was not a visible factor in the national campaign.

The issue did appear in a few individual contests. Most conspicuous was the effort by Liberal Mel Hurtig in Edmonton, mentioned earlier. His opponent, Conservative Marcel Lambert, passed the foreign investment issue off as of no consequence and won handily. Elsewhere, especially in Ontario, a few candidates tried to raise the issue but to little avail, either because of lack of public interest or the unwillingness of opponents to rise to the bait. The CIC tried to promote the issue around Toronto and succeeded in getting a number of candidates to endorse a modified version of their program, specifically, that a change in national policy is needed and that "Canadian ownership is likely to produce more and better quality jobs, a better standard of living and lower taxes" than foreign ownership of industry.[70] The position was endorsed by seven Liberals and fifteen Conservatives, indicating that at least in that area many Conservatives wished to project a strong nationalist position. However, the endorsement by a substantial number from both parties underscores the general lack of clear differentiation.

The campaign therefore contributes little to our picture of the differences between the party positions. But it does suggest some ideas about the role of the subject in the political process. The chief reason given by most Canadians I interviewed for its minor role in the campaign was that it ranked low in the public view of issues. Equally important would seem to be the problems for the major parties in making it an effective political issue. The lack of major differences between them precluded the possibility of establishing a basis for strong argumentation. At the same time, the wide differences of opinion within the parties could have created difficulties and embarrassments in attempts to make it a major campaign subject. The fact that Kaplan in Toronto was advocating screening all investments and that Hurtig in Edmonton was pressing the yet stronger CIC line was troublesome for Trudeau, who was committed to the limited takeover screening proposal. Fortunately, the Conservatives could not afford to make any hay from this disunity as the division in their own ranks between conservative Lambert and the fifteen candidates who endorsed the CIC statement noted above promised equal embarrassment if the issue were to be escalated in the election.

Yet another deterrent is what might be called the politics of nationalism. To what degree and in what form is it effective in a country like Canada to make an election issue out of a question involving nationalistic feelings? The historical experience cited above records the "success" of the Conservatives in three such cases and, contrariwise, the failure of the Liberals. But the degree of true success must be questioned in light of the limited time during which the Conservatives held power and the legacy of the nationalistic commitment. The Conservative efforts to stop the arming of Bomarc missiles with atomic warheads (under Diefenbaker) proved untenable, for example.

A little speculation indicates the potential hazards in the present situation. Suppose the Conservatives had tried in 1972 to push hard on a stronger nationalistic foreign investment policy. The Liberals might have felt impelled to match or outdo them. Would they want to appear less concerned with the future of Canadian nationhood? So the issue could have been escalated to the point where both parties would be making promises of strong nationalistic policies which ran counter to their true beliefs and would be embarrassing once elected. This, of course, is speculative but it is a line of thinking which the parties have to consider because of the emotionalism associated with the foreign investment issue.

What can we discern from all this about the differences between the parties? Philosophically it would appear that the Conservatives have somewhat less inclination than the Liberals to government intervention in the economy and, historically at least, a somewhat more protective nationalistic orientation. The opportunism of both parties seeking competitive advantage will lead them to some effort to differentiate their positions, although their essential conservatism, along with the specific aspects of the issues just noted, will hold their positions within moderate limits. This pattern of differentiation fits what we have seen in the recent past. Assuming it is valid, one would expect that the two parties would continue to push slightly different approaches —the Liberals giving more emphasis to the direct influence on the operations of foreign firms and the Conservatives stressing more the general indirect influences—but both essentially moving in the same moderate nationalistic range.

Future Attitudes

At the start of this section I observed that the recent trend toward less favorable views of foreign investment was one of the few clear-cut facts of the present Canadian situation. The other attitudinal elements discussed here—differences among regions and population groups and the components of the attitudes—present a more complex, less well-defined pattern.

In terms of the future, these characteristics are reversed. The diversity of individual views seems relatively certain to persist along much the same ranges one can see today—the more favorable views of businessmen, the emphasis on control, etc. But the overall trend is difficult if not impossible to predict. As we have seen, the reasons for the recent changes are not clear, probably having less relation to the actual volume and behavior of foreign investment in Canada than to opinion leadership, general feelings toward the United States, and other environmental factors. Therefore we have little basis for predicting the overall trend of attitudes.

The trend will, however, be of great importance in the evolution of national policy because recent experience indicates that the strength of public interest is a prime motivation for government action on foreign investment. The following comments by Edgar Benson, former Minister of Finance, are an indication of the sensitivity of government leaders to public sentiment:

I do think that if you are going to have relative satisfaction of the Canadian people in the long run, you are going to have to move gradually toward a greater degree of Canadian ownership . . . there is a great upward surge of nationalism all over the world and it is not just in Canada. You move to a stage where people are resentful. They think they're not getting a fair return out of the assets of their country and I think that feeling has gradually been developing in Canada. . . .[71]

It is widely believed in Canada that the stiffening of attitudes on foreign investment policy in the Liberal government has occurred largely because of public opinion pressures against inertia and real resistance by strong influences favoring an open investment policy. Thus, if concern over foreign companies continues to grow, there will be pressure for further action. But if the movement toward less favorable views has reached its peak, politicians will shift direction. At least a modest amount of speculation about factors affecting the course of attitudes is therefore in order.

The degree of control of Canadian industry by foreign investment is not likely to increase much more because of deterrents within Canada and discouragement of foreign investment by U.S. policies (e.g., DISC, investment restraints, and results of labor pressures against the "export of jobs"). In addition, the performance of the firms is likely to be more satisfactory both because of increasing sensitivity of the firms to Canadian interests and measures taken by Canadians. The changes in the concrete facts of foreign investment are therefore likely to provide less basis for adverse attitudes.

The course of general relations with the United States, a major variable affecting attitudes on foreign investment, is not at all clear now. The sources of current strain, ranging from the Vietnam War through the balance of payments measures, may well pass. But new frictions are probable. A major change in relations between the two nations is underway. Prime Minister Trudeau announced after his December 1971 meeting with President Nixon that the latter had made a "fantastically new" statement in assuring that the United States recognized fully Canada's right to determine its internal policies independently. While Trudeau interpreted this as beneficial to Canada, many observers feel this interpretation was essentially for internal political consumption. They see the real implications in the context of Nixon's treatment of Canada in trade and economic matters to mean that the days of the "special relationship" between the United States and Canada are past, that henceforth the United Sates will deal more firmly and less favorably with Canada.

One can find statements by U.S. officials which are quite explicit to this effect. For example, Paul Volcker, Undersecretary of the Treasury, said in a speech to Canadian businessmen: "We did not have the view, which I may suspect some Canadians may have had, that automatically everything the United States does immediately provides exemption for Canada."[72] His prescription for the future—"a wider, more mature relationship"— is eloquent, but in concrete terms it means hard-nosed bargaining by a U.S. government which is readily seen to be turning inward with greater concern for domestic problems and less leeway or inclination to help solve the problems of others. External Affairs Minister Mitchell Sharp has accepted this outlook as well: "To the extent that the concept of the 'special relationship' reflects an objective reality, it will continue to be valid. To the extent, on the other hand, that it denotes special arrangements between Canada and the United States, its currency is likely to diminish on both sides of the border."[73]

The change in relationship leading, as Sharp predicts, to the United States being "an even tougher bargaining partner than in the past" in areas of conflicting interests may result in aggravation of Canadian attitudes. The Canadian-American Committee, a responsible group of business, labor, and agricultural leaders from both countries, predicts that differences between the nations will grow deeper in the 1970s.[74] If disputes do intensify, the multinational firms would often be involved in economic issues between the nations, and feelings toward them would suffer as a consequence.

Another source of possible adverse feelings is the course of basic Canadian nationalistic attitudes. There may well be a growing consciousness of the distinct possibility that George Grant's assessment is correct, that if Canada has not already disappeared as a nation, it is close to doing so—what the Davey Committee described as "creeping continentalism" in its study of mass media.[75] We have already noted various substantive evidence of this process, as well as the opinions of such leaders as Pierre Trudeau which fit such a characterization. If nationalism really has an emotional force approaching that of religious fervor, which scholars in the field believe, it would not be surprising to find the attitudes supporting it aroused to perhaps their greatest vigor when the substantive base for the survival of the realities of nationhood was actually or apparently in the process of being broken.

Notes

1. Toronto *Daily Star,* February 12, 1972.
2. J. Alex Murray and Mary C. Gerace, "Canadian Attitudes toward the U.S. Presence," *Public Opinion Quarterly, Fall* 1972, p. 390; and Toronto *Daily Star,* December 30, 1972.
3. John Fayerweather, "Elite Attitudes toward Foreign Firms," *International Studies Quarterly,* December 1972, pp. 472–90.
4. Toronto *Globe and Mail,* November 16, 1972.
5. Robert L. Perry, *Galt, U.S.A.* (Toronto: The Financial Post, 1971), p. 106.
6. House of Commons *Debates,* November 18, 1971, p. 9,667.
7. *Debates,* May 8, 1972, p. 2,001.
8. Peter C. Newman, *The Distemper of Our Times* (Toronto: McClelland & Stewart, 1968), pp. 225, 418–23.
9. Fayerweather, *op. cit.*
10. Murray, *op. cit.,* p. 392.
11. Royal Commission on Canada's Economic Prospects, *Final*

Report (Ottawa: Queen's Printer, 1958), p. 22; and Task Force on the Structure of Canadian Industry, *Foreign Ownership and the Structure of Canadian Industry* (Ottawa: Privy Council Office, 1968), p. 121.

12. *Foreign Direct Investment in Canada* (Ottawa: Government of Canada, 1972), p. 416.

13. *Minutes,* Standing Committee on Finance, Trade, and Economic Affairs, Fourth Session, Twenty-eighth Parliament, June 13, 1972, p. 16.

14. House of Commons *Debates,* April 24, 1972, p. 1,576.

15. Toronto *Daily Star,* May 8, 1972.

16. *Debates,* December 9, 1971, p. 10,313.

17. Toronto *Daily Star,* December 4, 1971.

18. Toronto *Daily Star,* December 29, 1971.

19. Toronto *Daily Star,* April 12, 1972.

20. Toronto *Daily Star,* October 25, 1972.

21. Toronto *Daily Star,* October 9, 1972.

22. Toronto *Daily Star,* September 30, 1972.

23. Toronto *Daily Star,* October 4, 1972.

24. Toronto *Daily Star,* October 26, 1972.

25. *Lament for a Nation* (Toronto: McClelland & Stewart, 1965).

26. *Ibid.,* p. 90.

27. *Ibid.,* p. 63.

28. *Ibid.,* pp. 86–87.

29. Abraham Rotstein and Gary Lax, eds., *Independence, The Canadian Challenge* (Toronto: Committee for an Independent Canada, 1972), p. 25.

30. Toronto *Daily Star,* July 10, 1972.

31. Rotstein, *op. cit.,* p. 255.

32. Pierre Elliott Trudeau, *Federalism and the French Canadians* (Toronto: Macmillan, 1968), pp. 200, 211.

33. *Ibid.,* p. 196.

34. Trudeau, *Conversations with Canadians* (Toronto: University of Toronto Press, 1972), pp. 171-72.

35. Trudeau, *Federalism,* p. 177.

36. *Ibid.,* pp. 178-79, and Bruce Thordarson, *Trudeau and Foreign Policy* (Toronto: Oxford University Press, 1972), pp. 64–65.

37. Toronto *Daily Star,* May 6, 1972.

38. *Foreign Direct Investment,* p. 403.

39. "Foreign Investment in Canada," *Columbia Journal of World Business,* November–December, 1972, p. 24.

40. *International Perspectives,* Autumn 1972.

41. Dave Godfrey and Mel Watkins, eds., *Gordon to Watkins to You* (Toronto: New Press, 1970), p. 6.

42. Toronto *Globe and Mail,* August 21, 1972.

43. *Policy Resolutions* (Toronto: Committe for an Independent Canada, 1972), p. 2.

44. Walter Gordon, *A Choice for Canada* (Toronto: McClelland & Stewart, 1966).

45. "How Sovereign Is Canada's Economy?" *Reader's Digest,* October, 1972, p. 77.

46. Calgary *Herald,* November 16, 1971, and Toronto *Globe and Mail,* February 14, 1972.

47. Peter C. Dobell, *Canada's Search for New Roles* (Toronto: Oxford University Press, 1972), p. 78.

48. House of Commons *Debates,* November 4, 1971, p. 9,329.

49. Perry, *op. cit.*

50. Toronto *Globe and Mail,* November 17, 1971.

51. *Report of the Special Senate Committee on the Mass Media,* Vol. 1 (Ottawa: Government of Canada, 1970).

52. *Lament for a Nation,* p. 18.

53. *Ibid.,* p. 52.

54. Dobell, *op. cit.,* p. 81.

55. Toronto *Daily Star,* June 6, 1972.

56. John Fayerweather, "Attitudes of British and French Elite Groups toward Foreign Companies," *MSU Business Topics,* Winter 1972, p. 19.

57. *Minutes,* Standing Committee on Finance, June 14, 1972, p. 37.

58. *The Vertical Mosaic* (Toronto: University of Toronto Press), 1970, p. 373.

59. "Some Bases of Party Support in the 1968 Election," in Hugh G. Thorburn, ed., *Party Politics in Canada* (Scarborough, Ont.: Prentice-Hall, 1972), pp. 36–77.

60. *Ibid.,* p. 48.

61. "Prairie Revolt, Federalism and the Party System," in Thorburn, *op. cit.,* p. 206.

62. House of Commons *Debates,* December 9, 1971, p. 10,322.

63. Toronto *Globe and Mail,* August 9, 1972.

64. House of Commons *Debates,* May 29, 1972, p. 2,638.

65. *Minutes,* Standing Committee on Finance, June 22, 1972, p. 32.

66. House of Commons *Debates,* May 2, 1972, p. 1,830.

67. *Report of the Committee on Economic Development,* Progressive Conservative Party Convention, September 5–7, 1967.

68. *Priorities for Canada Conference Final Report,* Progressive Conservative Party, October 9–13, 1969, p. 42.

69. House of Commons *Debates,* March 2, 1971, p. 3,871.

70. Toronto *Globe and Mail,* October 28, 1972.

71. Toronto *Globe and Mail,* December 31, 1972.

72. Toronto *Globe and Mail,* February 19, 1972.

73. *International Perspectives,* Autumn 1972, p. 22.

74. *The New Environment for Canadian-American Relations* (Montreal: Canadian-American Committee, 1972), pp. 39–44.

75. *Report of the Special Senate Committee on the Mass Media, op. cit.,* p. 163.

3 National decision-making processes

ANY CONCLUSIONS on the course of Canadian national policy must rest on assumptions about the nature of national decision making. The combination of political characteristics which determine the decision-making process varies greatly from nation to nation, resulting in quite different patterns. These differences in turn are important determinants of the types of policies which, as a practical matter, are open to a country. The relevance of these determinants to policies on foreign investment is well illustrated by the frequent favorable references to Japanese foreign investment policy among Canadians. The differences between Canadian and Japanese national decision making are so great that it is difficult to conceive that the Canadians would follow the Japanese model even if it were the most desirable one for Canada.

A host of elements enter into the Canadian national decision-making process, of which four seem most relevant for the present discussion: the role of government in business affairs, intra-government relations, government-business relations, and fed-

72

eral-provincial government relations. We shall discuss each of these elements in turn.

The Role of Government in Business Affairs

Deeply committed to private property and a free competitive system, Canadians have generally limited the role of government in business to overall regulation and support. To be sure, the government has directly taken on certain business activities in broadcasting, transportation, and public utilities. But outside this moderately large public sector, the economy has functioned with a quite limited degree of government involvement as compared with most other countries. The evolution of business has been determined to a very large degree by decisions of individual firms, with the influence of the government directed for the most part to major economic policies such as tariffs protecting manufacturing and support of resource development by favorable taxation and construction of communications.

In the performance of this function, government decision making has certain characteristics of which some Canadians are critical, but which are in fact natural concomitants of the role. For example, one Canadian observes that there is a policy tradition "to avoid awkward choices, to be nice rather than tough."[1] An official I interviewed characterized the government as "timid." Others averred that government officials are overly concerned with ad hoc dealing with current problems rather than taking a longer-term view. In like vein, a Canadian columnist characterized the Foreign Takeovers Review bill as a "traditional Canadian solution . . . faint-hearted."[2] While Canadians doubtless have some basis for criticizing their government, the significance of these comments for the present discussion is that they describe characteristics which are quite natural for the traditional government role in Canada. Expectations of Canadians have been geared by and large to a government which acted only when pressures required it do so and then only in a moderate manner, avoiding actions which would disrupt the main body of private enterprise decision making upon which the overall dynamics of the economy were expected to depend.

Intragovernment Relations

A corollary of the traditional mild role of the government is the limited experience in the Ottawa bureaucracy with complex intragovernment decision making on economic matters. In my interviews, several people observed that there was too much compartmentalized thinking in officialdom and that communication among ministries needed to be improved a great deal. This state of affairs is understandable in the context of the responsibilities the government has previously undertaken. It was quite tolerable, for example, when the active government role in industrial strategy was perceived as essentially confined to administering certain limited forms of aid and control over manufacturers. For the emerging role of government in constructing major policies and implementing their strategies, much more complex intraministry communication is needed. Progress in this direction is evident in the task groups for the Gray Report and the committees now studying industrial strategy, which include people from varied segments of government. The character and implications of this progress will be discussed in Chapter 4, but the process of evolution is at an early stage and adverse effects of the compartmentalized pattern persist.

Government-Business Relations

Government-business relations in Canada are closely related to the government role in business affairs. In the traditional pattern described by John Porter in the *Vertical Mosaic*,[3] business and government leaders were both drawn from the same small elite class. They were socially close therefore, and an intimate working partnership was presumed to exist.

In the present situation, this relationship seems to have

changed appreciably. Preliminary findings of a study by Craig McKie of the University of Toronto indicate that the current business elite does not have close social relations with government officials.[4] One hears frequent comments about bad relations between government and business. Among businessmen there is some grumbling about overzealous officials trying to assert too much power and making unwise decisions. Other Canadians feel that the business community is too uncompromising and antagonistic in its attitudes toward government efforts.

Historically there have been few ideological barriers blocking government concern with business affairs such as are found in the United States. But the present strains suggest a new mood in the interaction of government with the private sector. Rotstein attributes them to the emergence of a "homestead" psychology.[5] He likens the modern executive to the pioneer homesteader standing amidst his self-created domain, adamantly asserting that no one has a right to say or do anything which would limit his full freedom of action within that domain.

Substance for these characterizations can be found in recent situations. The government has proposed significant legislation on labor relations, taxes, combines, and consumer protection. In all cases, strong business objections were voiced. But it is significant that in each case substantial modifications were made to satisfy the business viewpoint. Indeed some critics claim that the modifications went so far that business has no justification in claiming that the government is not favorable to its position.

The upshot of this would appear to be that there is a growing gap between government and business thinking. The chief source of the change is probably the emergence of a new type of middle-level government official with substantial competence and a strong will to accomplish goals somewhat different from those of business or to pursue them by means and initiatives which are not well received by the business community. The fact that the ultimate decisions have been made essentially in line with business thinking would suggest, however, that at the senior level of government decision making a fairly good rapport continues to exist with business; or at least that politically and philosophically government leaders are not prepared to take directions notably at odds with business thinking.

Federal-Provincial Relations

The federal-provincial government relationship in Canada is unusual, representing probably the most balanced federal structure in the world. At a time when central governments dominate most countries, it is striking to find in Canada provincial governments exercising a high degree of autonomy not only in education and cultural affairs but also in economic matters. They have a large measure of control of natural resources through their ownership of subsoil rights, vast areas of timber, and water power. While banking is entirely under federal control, other aspects of finance such as the regulation of security exchanges largely lie with the provinces. In manufacturing matters, other than in broad regulations like the antitrust laws, the provinces have asserted as much initiative and responsibility as the federal government.

The federal balance is an unstable, dynamic one. On the one hand, there are indications that the growing strength of the Ottawa bureaucracy, reinforced by the emergence of problems for which nationwide solutions seem required, is leading toward greater assertion of central power. On the other hand, the provinces continue to demonstrate their strong capabilities for individual initiative, for example, in significant moves (which will be discussed later) in Alberta for new taxation of petroleum firms and in Ontario in the handling of foreign-owned companies.

The conflicting positions of Trudeau himself are symptomatic of the situation. His writings assert a strong commitment to a well-balanced federal structure. His actions as Prime Minister assure that he retains this philosophy. However, as an aggressive, imaginative leader, he has added impetus to the role and initiative of the central bureaucracy. He has been critical of the response of the provinces to his initiatives, as indicated by these comments in Commons:

At the last federal-provincial conference . . . I asked all premiers to indicate their views on (foreign investment) during the following months. I am happy to say that some premiers replied with specific suggestions, but I believe that most of them are in the position of the Conservative party, that is to say, they reserve the right to criticize government measures but have nothing to propose.[6]

Beneath the publicly visible division of constitutional roles and utterances of government leaders is another, perhaps equally important, problem of federal-provincial relations. That is the interaction of members of the bureaucracy. My interviewing barely touched on this subject, so no broad conclusions are practical. However, it was apparent that in the area of foreign investment policy, communications between Ottawa and the provincial civil servants have been very limited, and the general mood on both sides is anything but the smooth and willing cooperation in achieving a common end that some people feel is needed. Characteristic was the observation of one provincial official that the federal government never consults the provinces except under pressure and that the failure of the group preparing the Gray Report to consult them was inexcusable. Federal officials, on the other hand, say the provinces do not help in developing cooperation.

The trend for the immediate future would appear to be the evolution of systems and institutions which permit the Ottawa government to expand its scope and initiatives but to do so in consultation with and respect for the continuing power of the provincial governments. Demonstrative of this trend was the proposal by Premier Davis of Ontario in late 1971 for a system to bring the provincial governments into regular consultation with the national government on basic economic policies. The proposal had strong support from other provincial leaders and met with a sympathetic hearing from Trudeau, though it has not yet been implemented.

The federal-provincial relationship has a strong bearing on foreign investment policy because of the economic benefits involved and the wide differences in views among the provinces. As we noted in Chapter 2, attitudes in some provinces like Ontario favor quite nationalistic measures. Other provinces, notably Quebec and the Maritimes, are so hard pressed for economic growth that they advocate an open investment climate. The Quebec situation is particularly significant. With resentment against Ontario business domination as great as that against non-Canadian firms, the direction of Quebec policy is quite distinctive. For example, a 1972 measure required 25 percent *Quebec* ownership of securities firms, clearly directed at Ontario as well as U.S. investors. The increase in Anglo-French tensions indicated as a factor in Trudeau's 1972 election set-back can only augment this type of thinking. Thus a special part of this whole subject is the evolution of a quite distinctive Quebec policy on foreign investment, a policy which must some-how be blended into the overall national approach to foreign investment.

While the provinces have sufficient autonomy to take substan-tial actions on foreign investment policy issues, they are re-strained by the competitive implications of adopting courses appreciably different from those of other provinces. In response to Ontario criticisms of the Foreign Takeovers Review bill as being too mild, Trudeau retorted that the provinces were quite free to take a tougher line if they wished, and he criticized them for "trying to pass the buck to get away from the responsibility of limiting foreign investment, but at the same time they want to make sure we don't limit it too much at their expense . . . I don't think the federal government should at this time decide in the name of all the provinces that their industry would not have access to foreign capital unless the federal government said so."[7] But Premier Davis of Ontario had soundly observed that this is not a realistic position, that foreign investment control "cannot be done by any single provincial jurisdiction . . . it has to be national in scope."[8] Ontario has taken some separate initiatives in this area. However, it cannot go very far without running a serious risk of driving foreign corporations up into Quebec, which is more than anxious to encourage such a migration pro-cess anyway.

Yet, Davis notwithstanding, the provinces are not prepared to give up substantial autonomy to Ottawa on this issue. Quebec and the Maritimes will stoutly resist a stiff federal foreign in-vestment policy which decreases the overall inflow of invest-ment. And in the crunch it is doubtful if even Ontario is prepared to give the federal Ottawa bureaucracy power, for example, to screen all foreign investment and decide whether or not new plants should be set up in that province or another. All things considered, therefore, I would concur with the conclusion of Carl Beigie that "extrapolating from the past, the primary impli-cation of the federal-provincial issue for foreign investors is that its existence will ensure that actions taken by the federal government will be relatively conservative and gradual."[9]

Summary

Summing up these observations, one may say that the nature of current economic problems along with the growing competence of government personnel are leading to a stronger role for government in national economic decision making. However, the traditionally limited role of government in the Canadian economy, the associated strong sense of independence on the part of the business community, and the division of power between the federal and provincial governments sharply limit the capacity for national action. Decision making in such a context is slow, and the capacities for arriving at decisions are limited by the varied viewpoints involved and the balance of power among them. Decisions involving new directions of national policy are therefore not readily made except under the pressure of new problems or conditions.

Notes

1. K. W. Studnicki-Gizbert, "Policy Instruments," *Canadian Forum,* January–Februry 1972, p. 45.
2. George Bain, Toronto *Globe and Mail,* June 2, 1972.
3. (Toronto: University of Toronto Press, 1965), pp. 520–553.
4. "The Ontario Industrial Elite Study: Influence and Power in the Canadian Context," unpublished paper, July 1971.
5. Viv Nelles and Abraham Rotstein, "Canadian Business and the Eternal No," *Canadian Forum,* January–February 1972, p. 62.
6. House of Commons *Debates,* April 19, 1972, p. 1,442.
7. Toronto *Daily Star,* May 20, 1972.
8. Toronto *Daily Star,* May 12, 1972.
9. "Foreign Investment in Canada," *Columbia Journal of World Business,* November–December 1972, p. 30.

4 Industrial strategy

"**I**NDUSTRIAL STRATEGY" was the most popular buzz word in Canadian economic circles in 1972. Early in the year the Trudeau government promised that an industrial strategy for Canada would be announced soon, and in the months that followed everyone in and out of the government seemed to be preoccupied with thinking out the set of goals, policies, and action plans which would be appropriate for it.

While a few people speak of an industrial strategy as something quite new for Canada, it is recognized, at least in sophisticated circles, that the job at hand is one of rethinking economic policy rather than of developing an entirely new concept. Canada operated with a basic industrial strategy which remained virtually unchanged throughout its first hundred years. It had essentially two facets: the first was the development of natural resources to the maximum degree that market demand would justify, supported by construction of communications links and a favorable tax policy; the second was the development of manufacturing behind a tariff wall to serve the domestic market. While this strategy was successful in its intended objectives, serious questions have been raised both about the objectives and about characteristics of the economy which the strategy has produced. There is general agreement that the current situation and future needs call for substantially different sets of goals, policies, and implementing actions.

Although reformulation of industrial strategy has now become the focus of wide attention, even this is not as revolutionary a process for Canada as many people imply. The process had commenced over twenty years earlier with the GATT negotiations which started the movement away from a protectionist, inward-oriented concept of manufacturing. By the early 1960s, protection had been reduced substantially and, more important, a strong export orientation was evolving among manufacturing firms. This orientation was being actively encouraged by the government, which observed even in the mid-1950s that despite a steady rise of resource exports, Canada had continuing balance-of-payments and unemployment problems. However, the government has been constrained in its actions by worries over the ability of secondary industry to compete effectively at home and abroad. The present industrial strategy discussions therefore represent the expansion of a revision process which had previously been confined to fairly narrow issues, largely tariffs, but which is now perceived to be a very broad matter involving a wide range of government economic policies. Thus, while not novel either in basic substance or central direction, the 1972 review is a major policy-making milestone in its breadth as well as in the varied directions in which it may affect Canadian national affairs.

The industrial strategy formulation process is highly relevant to the question of foreign investment policy because, as we shall see shortly, at virtually every turn the approaches being considered have major implications for the operations of foreign-owned companies. The outcome of the questions being debated under the heading of industrial strategy is likely to have a far greater effect on the conditions under which foreign business operates than the limited number of actions specifically labeled as part of foreign investment policy. It is appropriate in this analysis, therefore, to examine the fundamental issues under consideration by Canadians as part of the industrial strategy.

Strategy Goals

The goals of industrial strategy being discussed in Canada

have a broad sweep covering all of the aspects of human welfare to which economic policies could contribute. In addition to the obvious objective of economic growth, they include the equitable distribution of income (along both social and regional dimensions), price stability, balance of international payments, national sovereignty and control of industry, environmental protection, and the quality of life. The concrete issues which are of most concern for our immediate purposes, however, center around two subgoals: employment and level of sophistication of industrial operations, which are interrelated to the major goals in various ways that will be developed in the following sections.

The preoccupation with jobs arises from the exceptionally large increase in the labor force which Canada will be experiencing throughout the 1970s. This condition had its origin in the combination of the high birth rate after World War II and a high rate of immigration at the same time. The baby boom of that period is now appearing in a rate of expansion of the working population which is currently the highest in the world. The expansion hit its peak rate in the 1965–1970 period when the labor force grew by 15.6 percent.[1] It will taper off to 13.3 percent for 1970–1975 and 12.9 percent for 1975–1980. However, the pressure for job increases in the next few years is compounded by the failure to expand employment sufficiently in the recent past. Against the 15.6 percent rise in the labor force in 1965–1970, employment increased only 14 percent. Unemployment rose from 4 percent in 1965 to over 6 percent in 1972, with much higher rates of 8 percent to 9 percent in areas like the Maritimes and Quebec. Thus, if unemployment is to be brought down to a respectable level again, the rate of increase of jobs must be greater than in recent years.

The high rate of labor force increase and current unemployment figures result in understandable worry among Canadians over the prospect of industry's providing sufficient new jobs. Concern on this subject is indicated by the two Gallup polls cited in Chapter 2, which showed that employment had risen from being the "main worry" of 7 percent of Canadians in 1967 to 41 percent, the highest-ranked item, in 1972.

Despite the wide acceptance of employment expansion as a prime goal, even it has been questioned by some people. Prime

Minister Trudeau himself, while recognizing the realities of public concern by rating jobs as his number-one priority,[2] has raised the question of whether Canada really wants as much added employment as may appear needed. He suggests that greater leisure may be a preferred option that would reduce total demand for work.[3]

The second major goal, the achievement of a high level of sophistication of industry, is related to both the standard of living and the quality of employment. Canadians have the fourth highest per capita income in the world, and they are anxious to maintain this degree of affluence. Political leaders are particularly conscious of the fact that the Canadian income level is some 25 percent less than that of the United States, and Canadians will not accept with equanimity a widening of the gap. Indeed, there is a strong thrust toward narrowing it, evident for example in the drive for equal pay between the two countries in the automobile and other industries. Thus a basic component of thinking about industrial strategy is that emphasis should be given to economic activities which have a high value added per labor unit.

Reinforcing this standard of living argument is the desire to provide employment opportunities of an ever increasing level of sophistication. While higher education in Canada has lagged behind the United States, it is catching up rapidly. As a consequence, there is an increasing outflow of highly trained graduates. It appears that the present industrial system may not be able to supply sufficient high-quality employment to satisfy this educational output. A recent study by the Economic Council estimates that in the next five years Canada will produce seven thousand more doctoral graduates than present job expectations can absorb.[4]

In recent years there has been a continuous exodus of highly trained people to the United States. This situation is distressing to Canadians both in the human cost for individuals who would prefer to stay in their home country and in the loss of investment in advanced skills which, if effectively employed in the Canadian economy, would contribute to a higher standard of living. Thus the strong desire to upgrade the sophistication of work in industry.

Major Strategy Areas

With these two basic subgoals in mind we may proceed to consider the main areas of decisions with which industrial strategy must apparently concern itself in Canada. In the interests of an orderly presentation, each of the issues must necessarily be treated as a fairly distinct matter in the following discussion under two broad headings: resource policy and manufacturing. However, it is well at the outset to note the high degree of interaction among these components. Chart 2 has been provided in large part simply to make this point. Down the center are listed the main components of industrial strategy that will be discussed in this chapter. The arrows and notations indicate important interactions between these components, which will be elaborated on in the analysis. For example, the magnitude of exports resulting from the priorities of resource development affects the Canadian exchange rate and thus the international competitiveness of manufactured goods.

RESOURCE POLICY

As noted earlier, Canadians have traditionally given first importance to natural resource development, with manufacturing receiving secondary attention. This philosophy has come under serious question, and by 1972 it appeared that a national consensus for substantial change in direction on resource policy had already been reached, as expressed in a number of written statements and some specific actions. The actions were still limited, however, and the degree of change which would actually be accomplished was uncertain. The new approach had two main components: first, priorities between resource and manufacturing development, and second, division of economic benefits from resources.

Priorities in Development. Strong arguments are being voiced in favor of limiting the rate of growth of natural resource development and giving a higher priority to the expansion of manufacturing industry. The point most frequently stressed in this debate is the fact that equal amounts of capital invested in resource production create about one-quarter as many jobs as in

Chart 2

Interaction of Main Components of Canadian Industrial Strategy

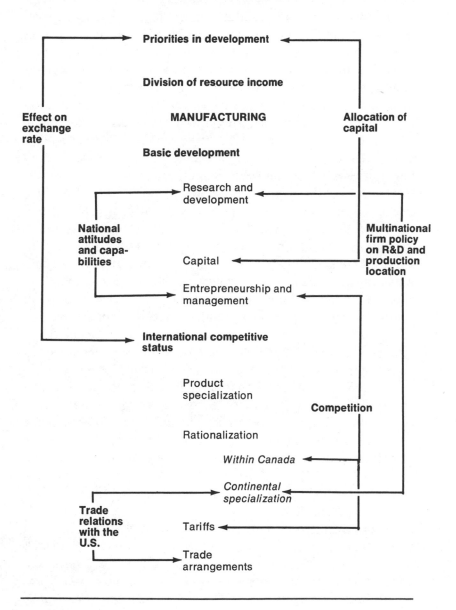

manufacturing. If a limited amount of capital available for national investment is assumed, therefore, the concern with maximum job creation leads quite naturally to a switch toward more emphasis on manufacturing. There is an opposing view to this thesis, which was the context of Trudeau's remarks mentioned above. The view is that resources provide a larger increment to wealth per dollar of investment and that it is the total wealth available to the nation which should be stressed. Ways can be found to distribute the wealth by lower taxes and other means so that all Canadians benefit either by greater income or more leisure. There is a persuasive logic to this view, but it has little audible following in Canada. The advocates of stressing use of capital for manufacturing are in vocal ascendancy.

A second point is the belief that expanded resource development, which would be largely to serve the U.S. market, would have adverse effects on local manufacturing in two respects. First, a substantial increase in resource exports with a favorable impact on the balance of payments would drive up the value of the Canadian dollar. The direct consequence of this would be to make exports of Canadian manufactured goods more expensive abroad and thus probably reduce their demand. Second, some of the balance of payments gains would undoubtedly appear in increased imports of manufactured goods which would compete directly with goods manufactured in Canada.

A third, quite conventional, argument is that Canada's resources are not unlimited and their rate of development should be restrained so that they will be available for Canadian use in the longer-term future. Reinforcing this line of thinking is a nationalistic reaction among many Canadians against U.S. expectations about the availability of Canadian resources. Some comments by MP Adrien Lambert of Quebec in the House of Commons give the flavor of the cause and nature of these feelings. He quoted Brice O'Brian, chairman of the U.S. National Coal Association, as saying, "Our government believes that Canada belongs to us as far as her energy resources are concerned," and summarizing some remarks by President Nixon to the effect that a major solution for the U.S. energy crisis lay in Canada's resources. The MP's assessment: "That is that. The Americans think that everything belongs to them. No wonder. When one spends one's time lending money to a neighbor, one finally thinks that the goods offered to guarantee such loans belong to the lender."[5]

While these arguments are highly persuasive among Canadians, there are substantial counterinfluences which will probably limit the degree to which they are applied in specific decisions. The demand for resources, particularly from the United States, is large and growing very rapidly, owing both to the depletion of U.S. resources and the rate of growth of consumption, notably in the energy field. According to one estimate, Canada's share of the U.S. petroleum market will rise from 5 percent in 1970 to 10 percent in 1980.[6] Since the total will have also risen, exports will roughly triple. Canada is therefore under significant market and official pressure to meet growing U.S. demand. Reinforcing this pressure are the interests of powerful companies, both foreign and Canadian, in the resource industries; they have a major stake in maximum output from their holdings.

Recognition of the pressures and opportunities has led some Canadians to advocate a different resource development policy. Typical of this group is MP Alvin Hamilton, a former Conservative cabinet member, who favors using the resources to the full but as bargaining vehicles to obtain benefits from the United States. Calling for a "positive nationalism . . . based on the realities," he describes "the immensity of . . . bargaining power" available in Canada's resources and asserts that "with dynamic policies based on our great natural advantages, the next decades can be the era in which Canada becomes truly Canadian."[7]

Some useful indications of the direction in which this aspect of industrial strategy may go were provided by the events in the energy industry during 1971. The first item was the response to a U.S. cabinet committee proposal that a continental energy pool be formed in which Canada would guarantee open access to Canadian resources to meet U.S. needs. The Canadian Energy Minister at the time, J. J. Greene, voiced a quite favorable response to this proposal in a press conference in Washington. However, there was a substantial negative reaction within Canada to a concept which was readily stigmatized with the label of "continentalism." As a result, Greene backtracked and rejected the basic concept in favor of the established practice of specific negotiations for each substantial increment of sale of

Canadian energy to the United States. It should be noted that around this time Greene himself was having a personal change of heart toward a more nationalistic position (like a number of other Canadians), so complications in his views as an individual may have contributed to the differences in his public statements.[8]

The second item was the handling of a specific proposal by a group of companies to increase the export of Canadian natural gas by about 3 trillion cubic feet per year beyond the 17 trillion already approved. The increase was approved by the Alberta Energy Board. After extended review, however, the Canadian National Energy Board, which has authority over all energy exports, turned down this request in November 1971. The stated reason was that the assured reserves of natural gas in Canada were too low to justify such an increase with safety. The facts in this respect were subject to substantial debate among Canadians, some experts in the natural gas industry arguing that there was more than ample excess capacity available to supply the proposed increase. It was charged in the House of Commons that the decision was based on potential needs for gas for two Ontario power plants which would in fact most likely be converted to coal soon.[9] This affair and presumably subsequent energy decisions involve sufficient indeterminate variables so that they are inevitably quite controversial. The negative decision is therefore indicative of a general direction of policy against substantial opposition.

These two events, taken together with the numerous expressions of opinion among Canadians, clearly suggest a shift away from the wide-open resource development and export policy generally followed in the past. The indications are that the merits of each future expansion proposal will be weighed with considerable care, and that Canadians will bargain hard for the best possible return of benefits either in specific resource deals or in other interests in manufacturing, finance, etc., recognizing that U.S. needs and Canadian resources put them in a good negotiating position. At the same time, however, the strength of the U.S. demand, the power of the interests benefiting from resource development, and the major income benefits available to Canada in the process are such strong influences that it is unlikely that resource development will be substantially restrained by any shift in priorities. The current Energy Minister,

Donald Macdonald, has clearly indicated that the government foresees a substantial rate of growth by observing that $50 billion will be needed for resource development in the next decade (not including major pipelines) and that much of this capital should be expected to come from foreign sources that will inevitably have a claim on their use. In fact, major new energy exports are virtually committed for the future in exploration and drilling development and proposed pipelines from new Arctic gas fields running through western and eastern Canada that will go into operation late in the decade.

Division of Resource Income. Accepting the fact that resource industries will continue to be a major component of the Canadian economy, Canadians have become acutely concerned with gaining a greater share of the benefits of resource development. This story has two phases, one of long standing and one quite recent in nature. The former is the policy of pushing for a greater degree of resource processing within Canada, already reviewed in Chapter 1. This goal of industrial strategy still appears in the current discussions, and a further thrust in that direction may be expected as a part of future national policy.

The new element is a drive for a greater share of the financial outcome of resource operations, with emphasis on taxation. Taxes have been geared to the traditional policy of encouragement of maximum resource development. The resulting tax rates have come under severe attack from a number of Canadians, of whom the most vocal has been former cabinet minister Eric Kierans. He compares the effective rate of tax on profits in manufacturing of 63 percent with that of 6 percent in petroleum and 10 percent in mineral industries.[10] Criticizing this as a very poor deal for Canadians, he has called for elimination of depletion allowances and three-year tax holidays for new mines, which would result in a sharp increase in effective tax rates.

While there has been no change yet in national policy along these lines, at the provincial level there has been a significant development in Alberta, which has 100 percent of Canada's natural gas production and 60 percent of the petroleum output. The Alberta government has initiated a vigorous campaign to capture a greater share of the profits of energy companies. The province is constrained by the existence of long-term concession agreements. However, it has gotten around this obstacle by offering producers the option of paying a new tax on energy reserves or accepting higher concession royalties which would average 21 percent compared to the present 16⅔ percent. Thus the Albertans (along with every other oil-exporting sovereignty in the world) will be getting a greater share of the energy dollar in the near future. It is estimated that provincial revenues from petroleum will go up about 25 percent.

Although Canadians in general may applaud this move as a matter of principle, as a practical matter the immediate gains will go entirely to Alberta. This is clearly not satisfactory to policymakers in other provinces, and therefore current discussion is also concerned with ways in which income benefits might be distributed more equitably around the country, perhaps through the tax and fiscal process or through some lowering of prices of energy to benefit all Canadians. A revenue-sharing arrangement worked out in 1972 between the federal and Maritime provincial governments for new offshore petroleum output in that area may provide a model for a future solution of this problem, although the basis for it in federal control of offshore drilling areas does not apply generally. The outcome along these lines cannot be discerned at this point because even the options are not well defined. However, given strong pressures and the obvious equity arguments, it seems likely that some solutions will be found in the direction of getting a greater share of resource development income spread among all Canadians.

MANUFACTURING

The elements of industrial strategy affecting the manufacturing sector are more numerous than those in natural resource development. There also tends to be substantial interrelation among them which complicates analysis. While this interrelation must always be kept in mind, it is useful to group the elements roughly into two main clusters, those affecting basic manufacturing essentially directed at the domestic market, and those which relate to the international competitive position of Canadian manufacuring.

Basic Manufacturing Development. Because of the priority

given to the objective of employment expansion, major concern is directed at the overall growth prospects of manufacturing for the domestic Canadian market. Some Canadians express substantial worry on this count. Noting the slow rate of growth in the past few years, they doubt the ability of manufacturing firms to expand sufficiently to meet the employment targets. More optimistic observers regard the recent past as an unreliable predictor of the future because of the general economic slack. Their optimism is derived in considerable part from the expectation that the expansion of the labor force will provide a self-supporting expansion of consumer demand. However, this is an uncertain assumption in itself, and it is clearly inadequate for an economy whose exports account for 25 percent of GNP.

The annual review of the Economic Council of Canada released in November 1972 cites data which are significant in indicating both the pressures on manufacturing expansion and the limitations in its employment capability. The council estimated that manufacturing will rise at a 6.5 percent rate per year through 1975. But productivity should go up 5 percent a year, so the net employment gain would only be 1.5 percent a year in manufacturing against the 2.5 percent overall annual rise in labor force noted previously. Thus manufacturing must expand vigorously even to provide less than its share of new employment. Furthermore, this vigor will probably be essential in generating income and taxes to support the service, construction, and other sectors which will have to provide more than their share of new jobs if the full labor force expansion is to be absorbed.

In light of current high unemployment and doubts about the future, the government apparently is adopting as part of its industrial strategy a policy of aggressive encouragement of industrial expansion. The 1972 budget gave considerable impetus to industry by reducing taxes on profits from 46.5 percent to 40 percent and permitting new equipment expenditures to be depreciated in two years. A strong dissent against this approach to fostering industrial expansion was voiced by the NDP and some Liberals (e.g., Eric Kierans), who felt that lowering personal tax rates to stimulate demand would be more effective. But the dominant Liberal thinking supported corporate tax reduction.

Beyond such broad efforts, the main aspects of an industrial strategy devoted to basic industrial growth are concerned with research and development, finance, and management.

1. *Research and development.* Research and development figure prominently in discussions of industrial strategy. Canadian R&D expenditures as a percentage of gross national product are appreciably lower than those of most other major advanced industrial countries (Table 7). This fact had already attracted considerable attention early in the 1960s, and Canada initiated a program to provide special financial assistance to companies for R&D work on new products. It is generally agreed that the program has contributed significantly to encouragement of R&D

Table 7

Percentage of GNP Devoted to Gross Expenditures on Research and Development (GERD), R&D Expenditures, and Manpower (Qualified Scientists and Engineers, QSE) for Ten Selected OECD Countries

Country	GERD/GNP 1963	GERD/GNP 1967	R&D Expenditures (millions of US$) 1967 Amount	R&D Expenditures (millions of US$) 1967 % share	R&D Manpower QSEs in R&D 1967 Number	R&D Manpower QSEs in R&D 1967 % share
U.S.A. (1964, 1966)	3.0	2.9	22,285	67.0	537,278	58.6
U.K. (1964)	2.3	2.3	2,533	7.6	50,350	5.5
France	1.6	2.3	2,507	7.5	49,224	5.4
Netherlands (1964)	1.9	2.3	514	1.5	15,700	1.7
Switzerland	—	1.9	304	0.9	10,954	1.2
Germany (1964)	1.4	1.7	2,084	6.3	61,559	6.7
Japan	1.5	1.8	1,684	5.1	157,612	17.2
Sweden (1964)	1.3	1.4	336	1.0	7,395	0.8
Canada	1.1	1.4	828	2.5	19,350	2.1
Belgium	1.0	0.9	176	0.5	7,945	0.9
Total			33,251	100.0	917,357	100.0

SOURCE: *A Science Policy for Canada,* Report of the Senate Special Committee on Science Policy, Ottawa, 1970, p. 122.

---

in a number of firms. But there have been criticisms of its administration in individual cases as well as overall doubts as to whether it has distributed its money according to a sound concept of priorities.

Two substantial reports on the situation have been made, one by a Senate committee in 1972 and the other by the Science Council of Canada in 1971.[11] Maurice Lamontagne, chairman of the Senate committee, has succinctly stated that "the committee concluded that the R&D effort of Canadian industry was largely wasted" because it was too small relative to the task, running about 1.4 percent of sales vs. 4.0 percent in the United States.[12] The report recommended a fivefold increase in total national research expenditures. The Science Council stated: "The main impediment . . . is the poor relationship . . . between government and industry."[13] It supported development of "a coordinated industrial strategy which recognizes the significance of innovation and gives priority to industries of high innovative potential."[14]

One source of criticism has been the amount of research done within the government. Of federal research and development expenditures totaling some $635 million in 1972, about half was used for "in-house" projects and only one-quarter for "out-of-house" industry work. Critics felt that the pay-out in industrial sales was too low with such a balance. Responding to this appraisal, the then Science Minister Alastair Gillespie announced a major policy change in August 1972. There would be no cutback in government work, but as new programs were launched they would be largely contracted out to industry so that the balance would shift over a five-year period substantially in favor of out-of-house work.

Another problem in certain industries—e.g., electric and electronic equipment—was the low level of government procurement compared to some other countries. There were also questions about procurement policy. Defense and capital expenditures, especially in the recent past, have been quite low and have not provided the foundation for industrial research that they do in the United States. In addition, businessmen feel that government officials have not given enough weight to research effects in key procurement decisions. For example, after supporting research on a communications satellite in the Canadian RCA subsidiary for some time, the government switched to Hughes in the United States for the final production contract, though with substantial subcontracting in Canada.[15] Likewise, although the federal government had financed research resulting in improved DC converters for power systems, a provincial government placed a sizeable order for comparable equipment from Britain to get a price advantage. While economic and other considerations may have justified these decisions, they do represent some loss of opportunity to further research.

The Senate and Science Council reports, along with such specific issues, have stimulated considerable interest and added to understanding of the situation. However, the problems are complex and Canadians are clearly far from defining a fully satisfactory industrial strategy for this area. Interviews with key government people in 1972 indicated that, outside the circle of those with a sophisticated association with the research field, the understanding of even the major options open to Canada was quite limited.

A critical difficulty in determining strategy for this area is the unique situation of Canada. With 60 percent of its manufacturing controlled by foreign firms and its market characteristics so similar to those of the United States, Canada is in a position to draw a very large portion of its technology directly from the United States with only minor R&D expenditures for local adaptation. As the Gray Report observed, this "truncated" type of manufacturing structure may well be an "efficient form of international specialization."[16] It is quite possible that Canada could have a technologically modern manufacturing industry with a much lower proportionate R&D expenditure than that in the United States. Some influential people like the 1971–72 president of the Canadian Economic Association, Professor Eastman of the University of Toronto, have supported the basic concept of Canada's saving itself research costs by reliance on R&D from multinational firms.[17]

Many Canadians are doubtful about the merits of this system, however, and there are further facts which complicate the analysis. Two intensive studies showed that the R&D expenditures of foreign subsidiaries were as great as those of Canadian firms,[18] but a recent report by Arthur Cordell of the Science Council has pointed out that significant portions of these expenditures do not directly contribute to the growth of Canadian industry.[19] A number of multinational firms farm out projects from the parent organization to Canadian subsidiaries. The results of the research then flow back to the parent firms, which may or may not apply them to production in the Canadian subsidiaries depending on their global strategic planning.

So far as strictly Canadian firms are concerned, it is not clear whether they generally lag behind the standards of other industrial nations in their inclination and capacity for research and development. Periodically there are significant indications of real deficiencies. Senator Lamontagne is highly critical on this count, asserting that managers of Canadian companies generally regard R&D as a luxury one affords when income is high, rather than as an essential investment to increase future income.[20] In the absence of clear assurances that industrial performance is satisfactory, Canadians seem generally to feel that significant improvements in the approach in this area are required as part of the new industrial strategy.

One of the chief options appears to lie in a change in the basic pattern of distribution of financial support. In place of the quite broad program of contributions to all sorts of R&D development in many industries, some current proposals run in the direction of deliberately aimed support for stronger specific efforts. The idea would be to identify particularly promising areas of industrial development and invest a greater part of government aid for R&D in major efforts to push these product areas. This approach would be related to the concept of product category strength, which will be discussed in the section on international competition.

Another major option concerns the relation of government support to research by multinational firms. One of the elements of the foreign investment situation which arouses the greatest adverse reaction is that some 50 percent of the government expenditures for research support have gone to multinational firms.[21] Former Industry Minister Pepin confirmed that government support covered 19 percent of R&D costs of foreign-owned companies in 1970 vs. only 7 percent for Canadian firms.[22] There is strong sentiment to cut off this sort of aid, but practical observers note that such a general policy would probably be self-defeating. Many Canadian subsidiaries are already doing good research which contributes to manufacturing development. In certain fields they are clearly in the best position to push further development in which Canadians have an interest, this being the specific explanation for the high portion of money spent on support of their R&D. A more likely outcome along this line, therefore, is a closer analysis of the way in which the government-supported research is conducted and utilized, probably with stricter requirements that results be employed directly for manufacturing development in Canada rather than being repatriated to the parent firm. Conditions of this nature have already appeared in some recent cases, e.g., the National Cash Register research plan which will be mentioned later.

But this philosophy may not be appropriate for another major aspect of the R&D situation. As already noted, in a number of multinational firms it is the practice to farm out specific research projects to the Canadian subsidiary with the results being returned to the parent. Major operations of this sort are still rare, but there may be a sound logic for multiplication of them in the future. We have already noted that there is a desire in Canada to provide greater employment for high-technology personnel. From the corporate point of view, Canada may be an excellent location for such facilities because the living conditions are considered by many to be superior to those in the United States. An analysis by the London *Economist* has rated Canada as the best country in the world in which to live.[23] Immigration from the United States has increased steadily in recent years, e.g., 19,038 in 1967 and 24,366 in 1971.[24]

In terms of efficient management of R&D on a global basis for a multinational firm, expansion of this type of research in Canada may often be sounder than pushing the type of research primarily geared to the Canadian market which the Canadians themselves might prefer. Thus Canada may find it is both more practical in general and, from its own point of view, in some respects more desirable to encourage this sort of branch research operation. At the moment Canadian national official thinking on this point is still quite uncertain. Arthur Cordell takes a rather negative view of the branch research structure.[25] But it seems likely that the issue will require considerable further internal debate before the government arrives at a consistent determination as to how it should be handled in the industrial strategy.

2. *Capital.* Until quite recently Canadians have always assumed that their internal savings were not sufficient to support

the rate of economic development they desired. This assumption, along with the general lack of concern over the degree of foreign investment in Canada, supported the traditional open investment policy. Furthermore, located next to the largest and most sophisticated capital market in the world, Canadians have found it convenient to rely on the Wall Street institutional structure to a substantial degree. Thus, in addition to a steady net aggregate inflow of capital, there has also been a substantial cross-flow of funds moving into New York and back into Canada. Canadians have invested through the New York market in a variety of ways while they have used Wall Street heavily for the flotation of provincial and other government securities.

In the late 1960s the balance of payments data led to an alteration of the basic assumptions about capital. It was observed that Canada had largely ceased to be a net capital importer. Indeed in one year, 1969, the country had a net export of capital. It is not yet clear whether this demonstrates that Canada is now essentially self-sufficient for capital needs. A major complication in analyzing the data is that a large part of the capital flows represent intracorporate transfers between parents and subsidiaries. Thus the variations over time may largely represent the capital budgeting changes of the multinational firms. The late 1960s were a period of slower economic expansion, particularly in the manufacturing sector, than should be expected in the 1970s, when greater growth will be required to absorb the labor increase.

Current thinking about the aggregate needs for the financial aspect of the industrial strategy is mixed. One finds some people observing with considerable confidence that Canada is now self-sufficient, while others still believe that provision should be made to assure availability of foreign financing, especially for major developments such as the tar sands or Arctic pipelines which require large amounts of risk capital. The Economic Council of Canada has predicted that foreign capital will again be required during the anticipated investment boom,[26] but a recent study by two professors at the University of Western Ontario argues that Canada has enough capital.[27]

In practical terms, this uncertainty about the need for foreign capital may not have significant policy implications. Despite the recent upsurge of nationalism there is little inclination in Canada to reduce the general free flow of investment across the border. Even the strongly nationalistic Toronto *Daily Star,* for example, had a recent editorial defending the value of the integrated North American capital market, entirely ignoring the implications of "continentalism," which would lead it to bitterly criticize such a philosophy applied to other aspects of industrial strategy.[28]

The financial questions being considered in the current discussion of industrial strategy tend rather to concern the capacity of the Canadian capital market to foster strong manufacturing development. The following comments from the Science Council report *Innovation in a Cold Climate* sum up the main points of concern.

Canadians have always tended to save money, and now have one of the highest rates of saving of any country in the world. A great part of these savings goes into bank deposits, pensions, and life insurance; we now have almost as much life insurance in force ($94 billion) as the entire population of the United States ($159 billion).

Either through these savings institutions or through private investments, we have a substantial investment in U.S. companies—about $560 per capita. We have larger investments in Canadian companies, of course, but tend consistently to avoid offering encouragement to the entrepreneur with a new technology-based product; as a nation, we avoid this kind of business risk.

Nor are the larger Canadian financial institutions noted for their enterprise in support of innovative industries. They do, however, supply abundant capital and operating funds to the more established sectors of manufacturing industry. The chartered banks cannot be faulted on this score; safeguarding their investors' funds is an important consideration, and they are legally prevented from acting as risk-taking merchant banks.

Risk-motivated venture capital companies do operate in Canada, but they are few and their resources are limited. In addition, they and their potential clients suffer from a communications gap: the venture capital companies are concerned—with just cause—about the management of possible new ventures; the Canadian entrepreneurs who approach them seem content with presenting a compelling case for the benefits to be realized, and tend to evade the management issue.[29]

These characteristics are often blamed in part for the large number of small Canadian firms which have been taken over by foreign multinational firms. In the typical case such as a firm described in *Galt, U.S.A.*, a budding Canadian manufacturing firm finds itself short of capital.[30] Exploring sources of additional support in Canada, it is confronted by conservative investors who expect the firm to accept relatively unfavorable terms to protect their capital. On the other hand, an aggressive U.S. manufacturing firm, anxious to establish a position in the Canadian market or to acquire control of new products or processes developed by the Canadians, offers substantially more favorable terms.

This sort of shortcoming in Canadian financial institutions was already the subject of attention a decade ago, and proposals for a government effort to overcome it have been evolving in recent years. After much debate, the government finally established the Canada Development Corporation in 1971 as the major effort in this direction. It is still too early to determine whether the CDC will achieve its intended purpose. It has an initial capital fund of only $70 million, but it is anticipated that this will be increased to $250 million through the sale of securities to the general public. The key question with respect to the CDC is whether a large, essentially public institution (though it is technically private), with the bureaucratic and fiscal-responsibility characteristics that implies, will be able to adopt a greater risk-taking philosophy than that of the basic Canadian financial community. The Science Council report is doubtful: "It is likely to be almost as conservative in its investments as the chartered banks."[31] The pressures to be conservative are underscored by the experience of the somewhat similar General Investment Corporation in Quebec, which made a number of bad investments and is now devoting much of its effort to encouraging foreign investment.

Even the CDC's first moves were subject to some significant adverse comment in Canada. It acquired the crown corporation Polymer from the government, an allocation of capital which Ontario NDP leader Stephen Lewis criticized as unproductive, asserting that the full CDC capital should be employed for new ventures or the acquisition of foreign-owned firms. Another key move was the purchase of control of Venturetek, a venture capital firm. The rationale in this case is that CDC can be more effective in providing capital for new enterprises through one or two separate venture capital firms than by making investments in many small enterprises itself. But one leading economist expressed the view to me that the CDC would have furthered the basic goal better by setting up a new venture capital firm rather than by taking over one of the all-too-few established ones. He also appeared concerned that CDC control of the firm might weaken its aggressiveness somewhat. This situation is further complicated by relations between executives of the venture capital firm and government agencies, and corporate roles of members of the CDC board.[32] While these relationships have not been demonstrated to be improper, they have given critics of CDC, notably in the NDP, ammunition and have complicated its early months. The NDP would like to see the CDC fully government-owned, not a part of the private sector.

In addition to providing a direct but limited increase in capital for Canadian firms through the CDC, Canadians have been seeking ways to expand the general flow of the domestic money into national equities. The main goal here is to divert Canadian money from U.S. investments into Canadian uses. It is generally believed that the rate of return on equities of comparable quality is greater in the United States than in Canada. In any case, Canadians do invest substantial funds in the United States which could usefully be diverted to domestic industry. Approaches to this goal include restrictive measures, such as limiting foreign investments to 10 percent of assets of pension and retirement savings plans as established in the 1972 budget, and incentives like the lower rate of income tax for dividends from domestic sources. As yet, in fact, there has been very little actual movement in this direction, and one suspects that is how things will be for some time to come. The major deterrent is the financial welfare of institutions and individuals, something the government will not tamper with quickly despite nationalistic pressures.

The other significant area is the evolution of the financial community itself. Canadians commonly observe that a more sophisticated and aggressive merchant banking function would serve their interests well. A natural evolution through assorted private enterprise efforts in this direction is under way. On the whole, the government does not seem inclined to take appreciable action to accelerate the process, though it is certainly favorable to it. The chief concern of the government in recent years has been more with security regulation. Control of capital markets in Canada is considerably lighter and less sophisticated than in the United States. There have been enough recent financial scandals to attract government attention. The resulting efforts to improve the quality of security trading may be said to contribute indirectly to industrial strategy by increasing the confidence of the general public in equity investments.

There is one item in this picture which has not received much comment in Canada, but which may be of some significance in the future. The move to restrict the role of foreign investment houses in Ontario has already been mentioned. As a result of the actions taken in 1971, new foreign firms can enter the field only as minority (25 percent or less) owners of Ontario investment firms, and there are restraints on the growth of those foreign-owned firms already in the field, such as Merrill Lynch. The charge made by some Canadians that these restrictions were essentially based on the desire of Toronto investment houses to protect themselves from foreign competition raises the question of whether the provincial government action has indirectly deterred the development of a stronger financial community in attempting to respond to nationalistic desires.[33] The Toronto investment houses objected to the unfair advantage which U.S. firms have in the size of the capital resources at their disposal. But it is likely that their concern also relates to the greater aggressiveness and skill of the U.S. firms.

To the extent that government regulations result in reducing inputs of this sort into Ontario financial markets, they deter the overall evolution of the capital-generating system. One should note that the same sort of question arose when the Bank Act of 1967 was passed; the Act sharply limited the operation of the one Canadian bank owned by a foreign investor (the Mercantile Bank owned by First National City Bank of New York) and limited future investment by foreign banks to 10 percent ownership.[34] The government asserted at the time that it believed that the presence of foreign banking was of real value in providing new ideas and competitive stimulus for the Canadian banking community, which was considered overly conservative and slow in the development of new ideas.

The implication of these actions would appear to be that Canadians have been prepared either consciously or unconsciously to accept some sacrifice of the quality of financial institutions as a contributor to manufacturing development in the interests of a greater degree of national control in the financial area. The actual costs and benefits here are so complex and subtle that it would be impossible to determine them. It is significant, however, to the character of the discussion of industrial strategy in Canada that this sort of trade-off is scarcely mentioned. The major issues whose nature can be discerned more readily, such as research and development, are sufficiently numerous and difficult so that issues like this one, which are more complex and involve more difficult questions of interrelations among decisions, are not receiving, and probably will not receive, any substantial attention for the immediate future.

3. *Management-entrepreneurship.* The preceding section has implicitly accepted the common belief in Canada that the financial system is at fault in providing inadequate capital for Canadian entrepreneurs. Some people, however, assert that the real inadequacy is in Canadian managerial competence, that there is no significant lack of financial support for entrepreneurs. The majority opinion among a group of experts assembled in 1972 by the Conference Board of Canada, for example, appeared to be that the real shortage was of able managers and not of financial resources to support them.[35]

It serves no purpose here to pursue this debate. The significant point to draw from it is the importance which Canadians attach to improvement of the quality of management as essential to industrial strategy. While criticisms of business performance might be glossed over if they came from other sources, it is highly significant that a group of business leaders such as those assembled by the Conference Board should emphasize this point. Ralph Barford, the president of General Steel Wares, Ltd., for example, noted—as an indication of the qualities Canada needed —the availability in the United States of "this fantastically able reservoir of management know-how and willingness to try experiments."[36]

In the current discussion of industrial strategy, there seems to be a widespread acceptance of the need for expansion of entrepreneurship and managerial skills. In the nature of the Canadian free enterprise system, however, there is little which the government can do in a direct manner to push development in this direction. The only real concern therefore must be that actions taken to achieve greater industrial growth do not result in policies or the construction of a bureaucratic system that may restrict the natural evolution of managerial skill now under way. As yet there is little indication of a problem of this nature, but if deficiencies in financing, research and development, or general expansion of industry created heavy pressures on the government for aggressive intervention, it could be troublesome. This is one of the key implications of Senator Lamontagne's prescription for management of the industrial strategy which will be discussed later.

International Competitive Status. The issues considered under this heading are closely related to those in the previous sections. All of them have an important bearing on the character of basic industrial growth. Dealing with them as a group, however, is consistent with a prominent element of the current discussion of industrial strategy. Historically the view of Canadians about manufacturing industry has been essentially parochial, with its key international component, the protective tariff, designed to insulate Canada from lower manufacturing costs abroad. There have, of course, been successful exporters among manufacturers like Massey Ferguson. But these are accomplishments of private initiative, not of any deliberate government policy.

Over the past decade there has been a major change in point of view in this respect. In present discussions, efforts to develop a manufacturing industry that is fully competitive in world markets has a high priority. Several factors converge to account for this change. Export markets are seen as a valuable adjunct in the effort to create new employment in Canada. Increased output to serve foreign markets would permit manufacturers to spread their overhead costs over a larger volume and produce with greater efficiency, thus benefiting the internal economy. And increased export income would contribute to the balance of payments position. Thus while the United States appears to be moving in the direction of greater protection, Canada is exploring ways to open its economy further so that the cost structure will be more in line with that of other nations and it can expand its overseas trade.

The Canadians have already made impressive progress in trade expansion. Exports of non-food manufactured goods rose from $409 million in 1960 to $1,300 million in 1965 and $6,171 million in 1971. Some $3,797 million of the rise from 1965 to 1971 was accounted for by automotive products under the Automotive Agreement described below. But even discounting that special factor, the export performance is strong. Manufactured goods, excluding auto products, as a percent of total exports have risen from 10 percent in 1958 to 16 percent in 1971.

Despite this record the Canadians are worried about future trade prospects for at least four important reasons. First, the cost structure and prices of many products remain above those of world levels. Second, the successes of the 1960s were achieved at a time when the Canadian dollar was running at an exchange rate of around $0.925 (U.S.). Since the dollar was unpegged in 1970, it has risen steadily, reaching as high as $1.02 (U.S.) in 1972. Such a large exchange rate change is a substantial deterrent to exports. This factor, it will be recalled, was an important consideration in the resource policy discussion. A supporting cause for concern, therefore, is the possibility that natural resource exports will expand considerably, putting manufacturing exporters at a further disadvantage through continuance of a high exchange rate.

A third factor is the emergence of strong trading blocs abroad that place independent Canada at a disadvantage. The dramatic change here is the entry of Britain into the European Common Market. The United Kingdom has traditionally been a major market for Canada. In addition to their historical affinity, trade relations with Britain have been cemented by the Commonwealth Preferential Tariff system, which gave Canada an advantage over the United States, Japan, and European countries in U.K. imports. The impact of the preference has declined with the general reduction of tariffs in the post-World War II era, and exports to Britain dropped from 15 percent of Canada's total in 1950 to 8 percent in 1969. Still, Britain is Canada's second largest export market, so the prospect that joining the EEC will alter Britain's trading pattern to the serious disadvantage of Canada is an important source of worry. To a lesser degree, similar concerns are expressed about the growth of trade blocs involving Latin America, the Pacific area, and so forth.

Finally, Canadians are concerned lest the logistic policies of multinational firms work to their disadvantage in world markets. A few firms delegate full responsibility for export control to their subsidiaries, but the majority to some degree, and many to a large degree, exercise control over subsidiary exports from the parent headquarters. The aggregate effect, therefore, of having 60 percent of manufacturing controlled by foreign firms is that a sizeable portion of export potential is subject to the discretion of people outside of Canada who are motivated by other goals than Canadian national interest.

Canadians are approaching the question of international competitive status from four directions, all of which are to some degree mutually supporting: product specialization, rationalization, tariff policy, and trade arrangements.

1. *Product specialization.* One of the current ideas with wide popular appeal in Ottawa is that the best prospects for Canada's export future lie in development of a strong position in a limited number of product niches. Interest generally centers on identification of product areas in which Canada would have a strong natural position, for example, built around cold-climate product design or its intensive experience with hydroelectric operations, nuclear reactors, and metallurgy. To meet the goal of high-value, high-technology production, it is assumed that products should be selected in advanced scientific fields to the extent possible. But more mundane areas such as the current success with snowmobiles are not to be ignored. Trudeau has endorsed this approach, challenging Canada to make some "hard-gambling choices" to implement it.[37] At least one government brainstorming session focusing on futurology in the selection of appropriate fields has been held, and the indications are that support of research, financial aid for new factories, and other official measures will focus to a considerable degree on a limited number of product areas to be chosen in accordance with this philosophy.

The whole approach is at such an early stage that it is impossible to judge its potential or feasibility. An obvious problem recognized by many people is that competitors outside of Canada will not be sitting idly by, allowing it to pick off the most promising fields for product development. Thus success will probably be dependent less on the specific areas chosen than on whether Canada has the competence to achieve a competitive edge despite the varied efforts of business firms and governments in other countries.

Implementation of a strategy of picking and developing product niches will require an effective system for selection as well as government support to provide whatever supplemental help is needed to carry the development process ahead. My interviews indicated quite varied ideas about approaches to such tasks and about their feasibility. Some felt the government should be a major factor in the selection process, while others believed the government was incompetent for such a role and assumed that private enterprise–free market processes had to do the job. As to means of providing support, ideas ranged from strong direction by government, with industry functioning in a sense as the contracting agency for government entrepreneurship, to a limited government role of providing incentives and facilitating financing in key phases of development.

Without attempting to appraise the merits of these ideas, one can note two characteristics of the discussions about them which are of prime importance. First, the differences in viewpoints are so varied and in some ways so basic (e.g., degree of reliance on free market forces) that it is going to be difficult to bring them together. It would seem consistent with the national decision-making patterns discussed earlier that considerable time will be required to evolve a policy, and that the outcome will probably represent a compromise of a relatively mild nature.

Second, thinking in terms of traditional government-business relations, one finds it hard to conceive a strong, sharply aimed product-niche policy. Perhaps the best insight on this point was expressed in the observation one Canadian made to me: "Any product selection policy requires negative product decisions." It is hard to visualize the existing type of government in Canada deliberately liquidating weak industry sectors or failing to support, at least to some degree, innovations which apparently have some promise even though they have not been singled out as *the* niches. The varied nature of constituents and of government leaders militates strongly against the singlemindedness that is characteristic of strong entrepreneurship.

In considering the prospects for this concept, the historical record is relevant. The Ottawa bureaucracy has rather limited background in this type of work, and the accomplishments to date suggest that much skill would need to be acquired. For example, a few years ago Canada apparently had a clear technological lead in the short takeoff (STOL) plane. Today that lead seems to have been largely lost because of the inability of the government and manufacturer to get together on a production program. The U.S. Defense Department and NASA both placed development orders for STOL aircraft in late 1972, with U.S. and European firms moving actively in the field.

In this case the manufacturer was foreign-owned (de Haviland of Britain), and some Canadians feel the difficulties are indicative of the disadvantages of foreign ownership. Others argue that the delays were due to the basic pattern of government-business relations together with a long strike in which ownership had little effect. In October 1972 the Canadian government did move energetically to meet this situation with a plan to contribute $62 million to a joint venture of Haviland and United Aircraft to develop a new STOL aircraft. It also took an option, good until 1974, to buy Haviland of Canada to give it flexibility if the condition of the company required direct intervention.

Quite aside from specific factors, however, there is an overall management perspective evident in former Industry Minister Pepin's response to criticism of the STOL program in Commons, which indicates the dimensions of the task for government if this phase of industrial strategy is to succeed.[38] While agreeing on the importance of market demand, technological leadership, the need to attract private sector participation, the role of government financial support, and the advantages of technology spin-off, he emphasized that "the name of the game in this particular instance is to try to bring all these factors together, and this is where the difficulty lies."

These thoughts raise considerable doubt about the prospects of the product-niche concept. In light of the active interest among officials, it will probably be discussed diligently. But substantial implementation is another matter. One thoughtful Canadian expressed strong doubts to me as to whether in practical terms the outcome would be much more than moderately preferential support for a few product fields in which the selection process and the main body of development came from private decision making. Another key official felt that the chief change would be that the type of product decisions the government was already making would in the future be made more on the basis of industrial strategy factors and less for opportunistic reasons. He thought that too often in the past, for example, Canada had taken on defense technology products just to have a "piece of the action" in a given field or to gain a balance of payments advantage under the procurement agreement with the United States.

2. *Rationalization.* The idea of rationalization as a means of reducing costs of manufacture in Canada is very popular in discussions of industrial strategy, but substantive moves in this direction seem to be progressing slowly owing to both practical and attitudinal deterrents. The rationalization idea originates in the assumption that much of the high-cost structure of Canadian manufacturing stems from the small market and the excessive number of manufacturing operations. The latter situation is due in considerable part to the fact that many foreign firms have set up plants in Canada to get behind the tariff wall. In the resulting so-called "branch plant economy" there are too many companies to permit reasonable economies of scale.

Views as to the importance of rationalization range from those who see it as a difficult but useful benefit in a small number of industries to those who feel it is the central concept upon which a strong industrial strategy should be built. The difference in views derives in large part from appraisals of the economic effects of rationalization. Those with modest expectations generally base their conclusions on a series of analyses by the Economic Council of Canada which have suggested that in a number of cases the average size of Canadian manufacturing plants is larger than that of comparable industries in the United States.[39] The studies further indicate that mere size of a firm is often not the dominant factor in the efficiency of production. It seems likely, therefore, that suboptimal scale of production is a problem only in a limited number of industries.

Those who feel rationalization has major potential look beyond the *scale of production* units to economies of *specializa-*

tion not only in manufacturing but in the entire operation of a firm. There are no solid research studies from which to appraise this line of reasoning. But there is a persuasive logic in the assumption that a company with larger volume in any given product line will have economies in R&D, staff services, sales organization, and assorted other functions as compared to one with smaller sales.

These differing views result in something less than clear definition of thinking among Ottawa officials on the importance of rationalization. But the general mood favors at least some movement in that direction as a key part of industrial strategy. Two main approaches are discussed: rationalization within Canada and continental specialization.

The idea of *rationalization within Canada* is a far more popular alternative among the stronger nationalists. The domestic refrigerator industry is often cited as a good example. There are presently some eleven producing firms providing a total output of about 500,000 units per year. This average output per company of about 45,000 compares with an average manufacturing volume of about 270,000 per firm in the United States. The Canadian tariff of 20 percent suggests the consequent cost differential, though, as indicated above, one cannot automatically assume that all or even a large portion of it is attributable to scale of operations. The solution proposed by nationalists is that all or a large portion of these firms should be merged with the sole existing 100 percent Canadian firm providing the nucleus of the new operation. Financing for such a merger could be provided by the Canada Development Corporation. Exceptions could be made under the Combines Act for this type of merger as economically beneficial. If U.S. firms retained in some way an ownership interest in the merged endeavor, then a more serious problem would be posed because of U.S. antitrust laws, though there is precedent for exceptions if the merger were ordered by the Canadian government.

The antitrust element and the disinclination of most business firms to participate in such mergers represent substantial obstacles to any significant progress in this direction. Major rationalizations through internal mergers are therefore likely to be restricted to fields in which multinational firms are not dominant. In fact some progress in this direction has been made in textiles, and it may also appear in pulp and paper. The textile business is an old one that is suffering from too many firms and antiquated equipment and management. After intensive study the government endorsed a program of rationalization and modernization which is now being implemented with considerable success. The pulp and paper industry suffers from somewhat similar characteristics, and it is being encouraged to develop a rationalization program which the government may also support.

A less radical approach to rationalization within Canada is product specialization within the existing structure of companies in an industry. This may be done by formal specialization agreements between two or more firms, a procedure which is specifically approved under the Combines Act where it is beneficial economically. Or the same end may be achieved by individual corporate actions responding to market forces. For example, RCA has acquired the color-TV-tube business of General Electric, the combined volume substituting an economically viable operation for two marginal separate efforts. Those who advocate lower Canadian tariffs (see below) typically believe that pressures of foreign competition would force Canadian firms into considerable independently negotiated rationalization of this sort.

The *continental specialization* approach is of greater relevance to multinational firms both because the U.S. antitrust implications are not a deterrent and because it is apparently more consistent with natural economic evolution and the prevailing business institutional structure. The essence of the approach is that multinational firms should assign full product responsibility or at least full production for given lines to Canadian operations with open access to serve the whole U.S. market. At the same time, reciprocal arrangements would allow full access to the Canadian market for portions of the product line manufactured in the United States. Variations of this approach have already been applied with substantial success in defense products and the automobile industry.

The concept of the Defense Production Sharing Program dates back to World War II, though the current application is guided by a 1959 agreement. The basic rationale lies in the technological and production efficiency of common arms design and production based on mutuality of defense requirements. Under the agreement there is, for practical purposes, an open border for defense equipment and a large volume of trade, with Canadian exports running around $300 million per year. By and large the system has been quite advantageous to Canada, with a cumulative net export balance of about $500 million and, more importantly, major technological benefits. Most of the exports are in high-technology fields for which the system provides continuing access to American R&D, which the small Canadian defense establishment could not support. Thus Canadian appraisals of relations with the United States like the Wahn Report typically give high marks to this example of continental specialization.[40]

But the defense agreement is unusual because of the nature of the market. The automobile situation is of broader relevance because it is in the general consumer product sector. While it has some special characteristics, it does provide useful indications of the feasibility of further extensions of this approach.

In the early 1960s a very unfavorable situation was evolving for Canada in its automobile industry. With all of the automobile companies attempting to make a full range of models in Canadian plants for a limited market, efficiency was low and costs high. A quite adverse balance of payments in automobile trade had developed and appeared to be worsening. The traditional solution for such a problem would have been restrictive trade regulations to limit imports of automotive products into Canada. Instead the Canadian and U.S. governments, in collaboration with the automobile firms, agreed to a continental rationalization program. The Auto Pact provided essentially that there should be free trade in the flow of products and that production of a certain portion of output should be guaranteed to take place in Canada. The product specialization concept was not incorporated in the pact, but it was an obvious component of the arrangement from the point of view of corporate efficiency. The firms assigned production of certain models to Canadian plants to supply both the U.S. and Canadian markets. This rationalization cut costs appreciably, one study indicating that the cost of producing an individual model in Canada by Ford had been reduced by about $100.[41] The prices of cars continued to be higher in Canada, partly because of a 12 percent retail tax and partly because of other factors, but the differential had narrowed greatly.[42]

From the Canadian point of view, the economic results have been extremely satisfactory. The adverse trade balance in automobile products was reversed to the extent that there was a net export balance of $300 million in 1971. Indeed the shift had carried so far that in 1971 the U.S. government, as part of an attempt to correct its balance of payments problem, started efforts to renegotiate the Auto Pact to permit the companies to produce a greater portion of output in the United States. Specifically it sought elimination of the "safeguard" provisions which required that companies (1) maintain the ratio of Canadian production to vehicle sales in Canada at no less than that of the 1964 model year, (2) maintain the absolute dollar value of Canadian content in Canadian-assembled vehicles at no less than that of the 1964 model year, and (3) raise the Canadian content in auto production by 60 percent of the growth of net sales and 50 percent for commercial vehicles sold in Canada. The base for computing this requirement was the 1964 model year plus an increment that had to be achieved by the end of the 1968 year. The increment for all firms totaled $260 million.

The Americans claimed that the safeguards were initially intended only to be transitional and that they were no longer justified in light of the strength of Canadian production. The Canadians, on the other hand, questioned the degree of that strength. They observed that the favorable balance in auto trade in 1971 and 1972 was due in considerable part to the good fortune that certain models assigned for production in Canadian plants had been star performers in the U.S. market. Down the road, the Canadians feared quite the opposite balance of trade conditions if one of their plants were assigned something like the Edsel.

The true significance of the safeguards was subject to considerable question in Canada. The importance attached to them by the Americans implied that they might be a controlling factor in future production location decisions. Yet former Industry Minister Pepin and some authoritative nongovernment observers asserted that removal of the safeguards would have little effect.[43] It seemed possible that governmental negotiators were making good use of aroused public opinion to achieve varied goals for which the Auto Pact provided bargaining material. Related to this was the widely repeated though unsubstantiated rumor that the United States was using the threat to terminate the Auto Pact as a lever to obtain a favorable energy deal from Canada.

The economic gains from the Auto Pact have by no means resulted in full endorsement for the basic concept of continental specialization among Canadians. One strong objection in principle is that most management decision making and substantial bodies of staff have been shifted from the Canadian offices of the auto companies to Detroit. This is an inevitable consequence of continental integration in some types of industries, and it clearly runs counter to the important objective of Canadian nationalism to retain control within Canada. This objection, it must be noted, is not universal. I was interested to find one prominent member of the Committee for an Independent Canada who did not feel real concern on this count. He observed that since the automobile industry was totally owned by foreign companies anyway, it made very little difference from the point of view of Canadian interest whether a certain portion of decision making and management was located in Canada or the United States.

An important point to perceive here is that the managers of the Canadian subsidiaries are likely to oppose continental specialization to the extent that the loss of control in Canada erodes their status or forces them to move to the United States to maintain it. The views of one government official in a key post provide a significant perspective on the interrelated considerations here. Although he had a substantial personal nationalistic sense, he accepted continental specialization based on multinational firms as sound in those industries where important economic benefits were possible. He felt that in these cases Canadians should not worry about the ownership-control aspects, that "you cannot trade off the standard of living for nationalism." He felt that "nationalism" in this case would be largely a matter of protecting the interests of a limited number of managers and owners of Canadian firms, and that that could not be justified.

Another source of concern was suspicion as to the distribution of economic benefits in an integrated continental business system. Specifically, the worry expressed was that intracorporate pricing in the complex system of exchanges of components and services within such a system would be adjusted to the benefit of the parent organization, with adverse effects for Canada. This sort of distortion should be policed by the tax system, with Canadian authorities ensuring that the proper portion of profits is allocated to Canadian activities. In practice, the difficulties which the U.S. tax authorities have had in policing intracorporate pricing arrangements even in relatively simple transactions suggest that there is a valid basis for some degree of worry on this count.[44]

Yet another reservation questions the soundness of any arrangements which set up special economic conditions for specific industries. The advocates of this view essentially believe in an open economy. They fear that provisions made for any one industry may have side effects on wages or prices affecting other industries that will result in distortions and other bad effects spreading through the economy. For example, the wage equality with the United States for the Canadian auto workers, which has been reinforced by continental rationalization, is seen as undesirable because of the pressures it puts on other industries whose productivity is not yet able to support comparable wage scales.

The most critical adverse attitude, however, lies in apprehension as to the effects of continental specialization arrangements on the future evolution of production location. In my interviews I found a widespread fear that in the course of time, labor and political pressures within the United States would result in a gradual shift of greater portions of production to U.S. plants. In light of the current attitudes of U.S. labor on employment effects of multinational operations and the sensitivity of politicians to their views, this apprehension is quite justified. Some Canadians cite as further reinforcement the experience with the agricultural equipment field. In the 1940s Canadian tariffs on agricultural equipment were eliminated, U.S. duties having been removed in 1913. Canadians apparently assumed that having Massey Ferguson, one of the major firms in the field, they would receive a fair share of the production effects of free trade. In fact, the geographical distribution of production has shifted since then away from Canada, with its manufacturing accounting now for only 6 percent of North American output compared to 12 percent immediately after World War II. Even Massey Ferguson now has its main plant in Detroit. There is no factual proof that the tariff reduction was the cause of this shift, but in the minds of many Canadians there is a strong presumption that it was. This presumption weighs significantly in attitudes and decision making despite its uncertain factual basis.

While government officials appear to be favorable in principle to the economic logics of further continental specialization, there is little indication of imminent actual progress. The somewhat apprehensive mood stimulated by the concerns noted above, particularly the desire of the United States to eliminate the production safeguards in the auto agreement, is a general deterrent. In my interviews I also found a strong undercurrent of feeling that continental specialization was too closely akin to continentalism, so that it was not acceptable as a general policy. Pursuit of the concept in specific cases was possible, but here I found discouragement owing to the difficulty of achieving progress in arrangements which would require a meeting of minds by a variety of people who on certain points would clearly be in conflict.

The type of specific deterrents involved are illustrated by the two cases receiving major attention today, tires and petrochemicals. The tire situation is roughly comparable to that which led to the Automotive Agreement, in that several competing firms find themselves making a wide range of sizes and types for too limited a market. The situation is substantially complicated by the conflict between the United States and Canada over export sales by the new Michelin plant in the Maritimes. The United States decided in early 1973 to impose countervailing duties on Michelin products, claiming that the financial aid given to the plant by the federal and provincial governments resulted in subsidized pricing. This situation virtually precluded immediate negotiation with the United States of a general tire rationalization scheme.

At the heart of the petrochemical situation is the fact that some products cannot be made in Canada at world-competitive prices because of the small demand, though they could be if the U.S. market were open to them. This situation is complicated by the opposing interests of various regions, notably Alberta, Ontario, and Quebec. The main petrochemical complex is in Ontario, and expanded production under a rationalization program might most logically be located near these facilities. However, Alberta, as the prime domestic source of raw material, is interested in developing the processing of petroleum products within its domain and would not quickly give up that option for the benefit of Ontario. And it is quite possible that Quebec would enter into the discussion, having available to it lower-cost petroleum products because it is allowed to import foreign crude, which is cheaper than domestic crudes. The federal government undertook a study with petrochemical firms in 1971, but no report has been released and no general follow-through on it was apparently under way in 1972. Former Industry Minister Pepin revealed, however, that the study concluded that greater access to the U.S. market was required for a strong chemical industry.[45]

The problems of applying the continental rationalization concept in the petrochemical industry are illustrated by the complexity of the considerations in 1972 proposals for a world-scale ethylene plant. Gulf has a 500-million-pound-per-year plant in Montreal, and Esso has two smaller plants in Sarnia, Ontario, all less than optimum scale, resulting in costs 20–25 percent above large-scale U.S. plants. Dow, du Pont, and Polymer proposed the Sarnia Olefins and Aromatics Project (SOAP), which would produce 1 billion pounds per year, a scale with costs comparable to those of major U.S. plants. But despite its basic long-run economic logics, the project involves a variety of questions. The plant would produce a number of products, mostly for local consumption but with some excess, for which access to the U.S. market would be required. There are no U.S. tariffs on these products, but freedom from quota restrictions would have to be assured by agreement with the United States. While the internal economics of the plant would be competitive with U.S. plants, raw material prices pose hazards. In 1972 the price of U.S. domestic crude was close to that of feedstock from Alberta. But anticipated new U.S. regulations would allow plants to import foreign crude at much lower prices, so some form of help by the Canadian government would be needed to keep the SOAP products competitive.

Then there were competitive projects to consider. Esso might present a plan for its own major plant at Sarnia. Since any new plant would result in Esso's having to close its existing small units, it would have a strong claim to prior consideration, and the SOAP project would be dropped in its favor. Alberta would like to see the plant located in its territory rather than in Sarnia. Its control over the feedstock gave it substantial leverage, even though the economic logics favored production in the main market area. Finally, Quebec was dissatisfied. The Montreal plant was operating at half of capacity, even though it had a major cost advantage from its imported crude.

It is indicative of the type of role the government may play in the evolution of industrial strategy that informed sources were anticipating that Ottawa would let the question of alternative plants be worked out by free enterprise processes. Once that stage was reached, it would step in to provide whatever concrete support was required to assure the financing and competitive status of the project.

Considering the complexities of the petrochemical situation, one expert suggested to me that progress toward continental rationalization would not be likely until the situation in the industry reached a critical point at which it was the only practical solution. Such in fact was the case when the automobile agreement was reached, and the greater diversity of viewpoints involved in the petrochemical and tire industries suggests that this logic is quite sound. Whether such a crisis will be reached, and how soon, is hard to predict. It is significant, however, that the chemical industry was under severe pressure in 1971–1972, with several firms, including the crown corporation, Polymer Limited, laying off workers and cutting back research. International trade difficulties, including the substantial increase in imports, were cited as a major cause for these problems. The trade deficit in chemicals had risen from $228 million in 1965 to $361 million in 1971. There was a prediction that employment in the industry would drop by 8,000 by 1976.[46] It is quite possible therefore that, at least in the chemical industry, the internal dynamics may result in sufficient pressure from the companies for rationalization agreements to permit progress there before too long.

A significant obstacle to progress in this area is the unwillingness of the U.S. government to enter into agreements assuring an open market for Canadian plants. The proportionate shift of production, and thus jobs, to Canada under the Auto Pact is viewed adversely in U.S. labor circles. In the prevailing nationalistic, job-protecting mood in the United States, progress might be hard to achieve. A major conclusion of a 1972 study by the Canadian-American Committee is that there will be considerable conflict due to job competition between the nations in the 1970s, with the "balance of employment" becoming as important as the balance of payments.[47] The importance of this point in Canada was underscored by the lead position (front page, right column) of the article on the CAC study in the Toronto *Daily Star* with the headline "Canada, U.S. Feared on 'Collision Course' in Hunt for New Jobs."[48] A revised Auto Pact and any future arrangements may have to contain a compromise satisfactory to the labor demands on both sides, notably assurances of limits on balance of employment and payments effects.

While continental rationalization of existing industry systems is impeded by assorted obstacles, the concept of encouraging multinational firms to expand by assigning continental product responsibility to Canadian plants seems to move ahead more readily. The Senate Science Committee also encouraged this concept. To some degree, progress comes even without government intervention. There are already cases in which firms have adopted the practice on their own. For example, IBM makes all of its printers for North America in its Toronto plant. There have been three major cases recently indicating governmental efforts in this direction. The 1971 decision of National Cash Register to establish a $16.6 million research operation in Canada is illustrative of these cases. The activities of this operation are essentially independent of NCR's present manufacturing activities in Canada. The products developed in the program would be made in Canada for domestic and export sale, and would eventually provide about 700 jobs. Half of the research costs are being paid by the government. Similar support for continental specialization investments has been given to the extent of $6 million of a $21 million IBM operation and $23.1 million of a $45 million Control Data plant.

It is significant that these three cases are all essentially in the data processing–computer industry. That industry as a whole has tried to push the government toward a general free trade policy, essentially based on the continental specialization concept. Canadians resist this as a general approach because they fear that the balance of trade and R&D work would heavily favor the United States and, most important, that the control of future development of this vital industry in Canada would be ceded entirely to foreign companies. However, the logics of continental specialization for the industry are just as compelling as they were in the defense and automobile industries. The outcome therefore is apparently that Canadians are moving toward that approach but on a case-by-case basis, which gives them a major voice in the decision-making process. This approach would appear to be consistent with the current mood of Canada. The only significant dissenting viewpoint I found among Canadians was that there were real risks that the new products planned for these operations might fail, and that it might be wiser to invest in more certain undertakings.

3. *Tariff policy.* Sentiment for a reversal of the long-standing national policy of high protective tariffs is strong in Canada. Indeed, some people I interviewed will be distressed to find this subject appearing so late in the discussion of industrial strategy, for they feel that tariffs are the key issue from which other changes will flow naturally. As a practical matter this is a minority viewpoint, most influential Canadians feeling that operational areas like R&D and rationalization require first attention.

Apart from this question of priority, however, there is widespread agreement that tariffs should be reduced to open Canada to world competition, with beneficial effects on both domestic costs and the evolution of efficiencies of national specialization. Concrete proposals for substantial tariff reduction are being made by prominent people. For example, Eric Kierans has proposed an across-the-board unilateral 10 percent reduction in tariffs each year for the next ten years, resulting in free trade by the 1980s. More selective approaches are advocated by those proposing rationalization plans. Their general concept is that internal changes should be made in order to make it possible for Canadian costs to come down to world levels, but that these changes should be accompanied by tariff reductions subjecting Canadian producers to competitive pressures from world markets for price reductions.

Despite wide public support, however, the route to lower tariffs will not be easy because of the large vested interests of protected industries. The very problem and result to which the low tariff arguments are directed—restructuring industry along more competitive lines—assure that many firms are going to be forced out of business or at least required to make major changes to survive under lower tariffs. This prospect inevitably generates a negative reaction. Its breadth is illustrated by the views of Dr. R. J. Richardson, president of du Pont of Canada, who spoke of the problems of several other industries as well as his own:

Dr. Richardson believes much could be done to retain a substantial portion of the Canadian market for domestic producers, although that is contrary to current Canadian policy. Other major industrialized nations are using this approach to their high-technology, capital-intensive industries.

The other alternative, increasing exports, presents important difficulties, at least for the Canadian chemical industry, from the point of view of scale.

If Dr. Richardson stresses that the alternative to the exploitation of external markets is selective development of domestic industry, he emphasizes that such a policy cannot be designed for the chemical industry alone.

A wide range of Canadian manufacturing is currently in trouble—chemicals, electronics and electrical appliances, farm machinery, rubber, aviation and pulp and paper. In addition, steel and automobiles are feeling the pinch of low-cost imported products.

These industries, by and large, have several things in common. They are high-technology, capital-intensive industries; they are competing with foreign manufacturers, which have the strong support of their home governments through a proliferation of nationalistic incentives and subsidies; and they are mostly subject to substantial economies of scale and lower labor costs, which inevitably encourages producers to operate a maximum-sized plant at as close as possible to full capacity through the exploitation of foreign markets.[49]

Dr. Richardson avoids the unpopular course of insisting on tariff protection, with its implications of high prices for Canadians. But he makes a strong plea for "support" by quotas or other means to preserve a full share of the domestic market for Canadian firms. Based on practical observation, one may extrapolate from this argument that such industries will stoutly resist tariff reductions since they are a much better-established and reliable source of security than the other prospective forms of "support."

Along with the tariff level issue, a question of timing also appears in the current discussions. Ideally, Canadians would like to see rationalization and other changes to make manufacturers competitive come first, followed by tariff reductions to add competitive vigor and assure that benefits of the changes reach the Canadian consumer. But most people I interviewed expressed doubts as to the realism of such a process. They felt that most manufacturers would not come to grips with the problems of cost reduction until forced to do so, and that the government in most cases was not able to push effectively for changes other than through tariff policy. The present government approach seems to be a compromise between the two extreme alternatives. It is trying to reduce tariffs very slowly so that industry can make its own adjustments, aided when possible by government programs. This approach lay behind the Canadian decision in the Kennedy Round of tariff negotiations not to agree to a general formula of tariff reductions, making only specific *quid pro quo* cuts. The initial slow pace of the specific cuts which were agreed to (1 percent a year) was in fact accelerated later as a government effort to check inflation, but manufacturers criticized the acceleration and it should not be taken as a basic change in tariff policy.

Another factor which will influence the course of tariffs is the locus of control of future negotiations. In the past the Finance Ministry has handled this function, guided by what one Canadian described as the traditional horse-trading approach of bargaining for balancing concessions. The opinion was expressed to me that unless the control (though not necessarily the actual negotiating function) shifted to those with a broad view of industrial strategy, the prospects for tariff changes of significant value in making the Canadian economy more competitive were slim.

The combination of wide public advocacy of tariff reductions and substantial blocks of industrial resistance suggests that movement toward a more open commercial policy will be seen in the future, but at a gradual pace. This in effect would mean a continuation of the trend noted earlier, which started with the first GATT negotiations over twenty years ago. External

Affairs Minister Sharp affirmed this prospect in his basic policy statement on U.S. relations described earlier: "There is no basic change envisaged in Canada's multinational trade policy. On the contrary, we could expect to be working closely with the United States in promoting a more liberal world-trading environment."[50] He looked forward to moving ahead with this approach in the new round of world trade negotiations expected in 1973.

4. *Trade arrangements.* A major current preoccupation in Canada is the effect of the evolving structure of trade arrangements among countries. Changes in U.S. trade policy, Britain's entry into the European Economic Community, some trend toward development of regional trade blocs elsewhere, and other developments have impressed the problems of trade relations on Canadians; and key officials in the government are actively exploring the options open to Canada.

The major problem which recurs regularly in industrial strategy discussions is the relative isolation of Canada. With the expansion of EEC, Canada would be the only major industrial nation without open access to a market of 100 million people. With exports running 25 percent of GNP and 27 percent of manufactured goods (1970), Canada's competitive disadvantage is a matter of prime concern. The Economic Council of Canada has given this topic a high priority: "There is the more fundamental issue of how Canada will respond to the 'new generation' of big industrial markets, big international firms and the acceleration of technological change. Access to a large market for industrial products will undoubtedly be even more important in the future than it has in the past."[51] The critical question seems to be (1) whether the general trend in the world toward evolution of trading blocs will lead Canada into a closer integration with the United States, or (2) whether Canada will form strong formal ties with one or more other groups, or (3) whether it will be practical for it to play something of a lone wolf game, gaining beneficial trading opportunities for itself in assorted relations among the various global trading groups as well as independent countries.

While the idea of close trading integration with the United States has strong supporters in Canada, including, as we have noted, some prominent groups advocating a common market, this outcome runs too strongly against the current mood opposing continentalism to be popular. The most that can be immediately expected in that direction will probably be the extension of continental rationalization discussed above. Thus the latter two alternatives would appear to be the most likely present directions for planned Canadian policy. This thrust of official Canadian intent is clearly affirmed by Mitchell Sharp's policy statement described in Chapter 2. Rejecting a basic policy of closer integration with the United States, he observes: "The object is essentially to create a sounder, less vulnerable economic base for competing in the domestic and world markets and deliberately to broaden the spectrum of markets in which Canadians can and will compete."[52]

Sharp's concept is a logical course in the context of the current direction of attitudes and thinking in Canada. The big questions, however, are whether it is feasible, and if not, what will be the actual outcome. The statement quoted above is followed immediately in Sharp's article by an enunciation of the main components of a quite nationalistically oriented industrial strategy (e.g., rationalization, the emergence of strong Canadian-controlled firms, etc.), vigorously implemented by "close cooperation of government, business and labour." He is probably correct in regarding them as requisite conditions for achievement of the objective and, in light of the uncertainties of their being achieved, the prospects for Sharp's basic goal are not promising.

One senses rather that because of Canada's relative weakness in trade status compared to the major blocs and its own internal decision-making problems, the course of trade relations will be determined more by external evolution and resultant pressures in Canada than by Canadian desires. Conservative MP H. W. Danforth portrayed this concern vividly: "The world is breaking down into blocks of potential consumers. I am afraid that Canada will find itself running around at the last moment trying to beg someone to look at us as a trading nation."[53]

If Canada finds the opportunities for export expansion to Europe and perhaps other areas unduly squeezed, it will have to make a major decision on trade relations, especially with the United States, in a quite different context than Mr. Sharp assumed. One course would be an inner-directed economic restructuring—domestic rationalization, etc.—guided by nationalistic criteria with limited foreign trade. J. L. Biddell, a businessman and treasurer of the Committee for an Independent Canada, has advocated such a policy: "We should be directing our efforts to make Canada an island unto itself. I believe Canada can become a successful 'Block of One.' "[54] The alternative, foreseen for example by the Canadian-American Committee, is that difficulties in trade relations with other countries "could force Canada to seek some form of bilateral trade accommodation with the United States."[55] In effect the logic is that when other alternatives fail, the "continental pull" becomes the controlling influence.

Prediction on this point is impossible because of the number and complexity of the variables involved—policies of many other nations, world economic conditions, Canadian nationalism, Canadian decision-making forces, etc. The best one can do is lean somewhat on history and somewhat on apparent natural directions of evolution. Both suggest that the Canadian-American Committee expectation is the more likely to be accurate. Past experience would seem to preclude an extreme nationalistic solution with its probable high economic cost. The natural ties and mutual dependence with the United States are so great that in a crisis situation Canada is likely to seek solutions with it, just as it did when the auto trade situation became critical. A key factor here is the substantial power Canada has in its resources to bargain for a truly beneficial solution with the United States, something it is much less able to do with other countries or trade blocs.

Overall, therefore, the best guess one can make for the future is that Canada will try diligently to broaden and strengthen its trading relations with many nations. But circumstances are quite likely to develop that will force it to work out closer trading integration with the United States.

Industrial System Attitudes

Laying out each of the major elements of an industrial strategy, as I have done, is essential for this study, but it fails to convey what may be the most important part of the story. The major elements, while posing significant problems, are relatively well-defined matters which appear to be susceptible to specific actions by government with reasonable prospects of progress. But the total situation underlying them presents a quite different order of problem which may be critical in achieving the fundamental goals of motivating strong job-creating industrial expansion, infusing aggressive innovating spirit, and making industry competitive in the world. The essence of this problem has been well described by Maurice Lamontagne, chairman of the Special Senate Committee on Science Policy.

In Volume II of the report released last January by the Special Senate Committee on Science Policy, we devoted three long chapters to the urgent necessity for Canada to develop a positive and coherent industrial strategy. This strategy should rest mainly on the production of a high flow of technological innovations especially in the manufacturing sector, either through an effective indigenous R&D effort, or the quick adaption of inventions made by others. This is a new vocation for our country. For the first time in our history, we have to become an innovative nation. . . .

In the past, we have had most of the time a passive strategy, merely reacting to changes in the external environment or in the technological climate developed abroad. In the early part of the 19th century, when we really began to expand, we reacted to British strategy and our main dynamic factors of growth were exports of flour, wheat, square timber and wooden sailships. . . . Soon after Confederation . . . a high tariff policy was adopted . . . to protect our infant manufacturing industries, which could then use imported technology to supply the Canadian market. . . . When the second technological revolution, based mainly on new resources of energy, on electricity, the substitution of non-ferrous metals for steel and the use of wood in the production of paper, was introduced in the United States, we welcomed the American invasion which was aimed at developing resource-oriented industries in Canada to meet new U.S. requirements and manufacturing industries to supply the Canadian markets with the products of the new revolution, such as motor cars and electrical appliances.

In spite of our traditional passive industrial strategy, we became an affluent nation. But there lies an important aspect of the Canadian tragedy: we are one of the few countries in the world which did not have to fight and innovate to become affluent. The other unique aspect of that tragedy is that we never really had to struggle to obtain

our individual freedom and our national independence or to preserve
the integrity of our territory. Our nation has become more or less
like the child of wealthy parents who never had to be strongly motivated to attain economic security but who has developed in the
process a feeling of psychological insecurity. And like many children
spoiled by their parents, different segments of our society tend to
make others responsible for the problems arising from their own lack
of motivation and their own insecurity.

While this guilt transfer process operates in many aspects of our
national life, it is perhaps nowhere more evident than in the economic area where it is used to explain our basic failure to innovate.
Some Canadians explain that failure by the extent of foreign ownership and control. Industry blames universities because it cannot get
the scientists and engineers with the type of training it needs. Universities criticize industry because the jobs it offers are too prosaic for
the highly specialized Ph.D.s they produce. We have our fair share
of good inventors, but they seldom want or get the management
advice and the capital they need to transform their inventions into
innovations in Canada. So they give up or they go to the United
States. The directors of industrial research laboratories privately
complain that their R&D budgets are too limited and that they do
not have enough access to top management but, in public, they ask
the government to contract out more R&D activities to industry so
that they can maintain or expand their own operation. Government
agencies claim that industrial laboratories are not competent to do
the job properly, so they continue to develop their own research
empire. Top industrial management blames its inability to innovate
on inimical government policies, but the government claims that its
responsibility is to protect the consumer against monopolistic exploitation, the workers against technological change which destroys jobs,
and the public against industrial pollution. Pure scientists in universities and government want more public money but they are completely opposed to any kind of public control. Thus, everybody
involved in the innovation process agrees that we have badly failed
in this area in Canada, but blames others for this collective failure. . . .

The Senate Committee has found that most of the above criticisms
that Canadians are throwing at each other during the present debate
on industrial strategy and science policy are justified. We expect,
however, that as long as the debate continues along these lines, it
will become completely sterile; to be profitable, it has to develop as
a process of parallel but complementary self-examinations with the
objective of arriving at cooperative and collective solutions. We have,
it appears, many problem finders; what we need are more problem
solvers. If the university, the industrial and the government sectors

do not begin now to go through the problem solving process to see what each of them can do to improve the climate for innovation in Canada and to develop effectively the cooperative action they must take to attain that goal, we will never become an innovative nation.[56]

Lamontagne's analysis suggests that achievement of the industrial strategy goals will require a virtual social revolution— a broad change in thinking, values and behavior among businessmen and others, including government officials who affect their performance. The heart of this conclusion lies in Lamontagne's picture of a system in which various components are each blaming the other for basic deficiencies. The self-reinforcing inertia of such a system can only be changed by major new influences. Can Canada accomplish that sort of revolution? On the basis of past experience one must be doubtful, partly because the present system is so intimately entwined with the general Canadian culture, but mostly because the capacity for inducing change seems so modest relative to the task.

The impetus for a revolutionary change in the industrial system would have to come from the government. It would require forceful direction and pervasive implementation by government officials. The Senate committee's prescription as outlined by Lamontagne indicates the nature of the official and semiofficial intervention that would be involved:

We felt that major conversion of most of our secondary manufacturing industries was needed in order to build up and use an effective innovative capacity and that this complicated undertaking should be accomplished in two stages:

In the first phase, the principle of democracy should be used so as to benefit from the practical experience of both business and labour leaders who have had to live with the problem of scale for many years. They know best the complicated technical, managerial, and job adjustments that maximum efficiency will require in their industries. . . . Each major secondary manufacturing industry, with its immediately related sectors, would be asked to set up a task force and prepare a reorganization plan incorporating desirable mergers and product specialization schemes together with their employment and regional implications and the form of government assistance required.

The Minister of Industry, Trade and Commerce should take the initiative and should appoint an impartial full-time chairman and a small secretariat for each task force. . . . The role of the chairman and the secretariat would not be to direct and control the work of the task force but to make sure that it does its job on time and to help if requested. The plan proposed would be the exclusive responsibility of the task force itself and would be presented to the minister by the chairman along with his own reaction.

The first stage would offer several advantages. Many task forces could work in parallel. They could consult with each other on matters of common interest or grey areas and thus this large-scale national undertaking could be completed much more rapidly and effectively. Industry and labour could not complain that unrealistic programs had been imposed on them without proper consultation.

Canadian subsidiaries, as members of these task forces, would have an excellent opportunity to show how they could fit better into the Canadian scene and make a greater contribution to the national objective of fostering technological innovations. Since the plans prepared by the private sector would be presented to public authorities more or less at the same time, they would provide both in detail and in broad outline a view of what has to be done in the whole sector of secondary manufacturing in Canada.

The second stage would consist of a government review of the plans in the light of the requirements of the public interest, particularly economic efficiency, innovative potentiality, and international competitiveness.[57]

This idea is similar in certain ways to the indicative planning system adopted by France, which has had only limited success there.[58] It would not seem likely to accomplish as much in Canada's society, which is less attuned to centralized planning. Indeed, one wonders whether the rather ponderous system contemplated might not deter the development of the innovative spirit desired.

The Senate committee plan is useful in posing the basic question of what the role of government in the industrial strategy should be. The indications from current experience are that the present capabilities would not be adequate to handle effectively a role of the magnitude proposed by the committee. The modest efforts in recent years toward a more active role have not been too successful. An overhauling of the program to help economically depressed regions is now under way because it has not been particularly productive, one study showing that eleven of eighteen grants under the program had no actual influence on location of plants.[59] As already noted, the research grant program is being reassessed because of dissatisfaction with its

effects. Provincial governments have encountered serious problems with some major industrial operations they have pro-
moted.[60] Such problems do not indicate exceptional shortcomings, for one finds comparable experiences in other countries as
officials develop their competence. But the evidence does cast
doubt on the ability of the Canadian government to lead a
major revolution in the industrial system.

It would appear that government leaders recognize their limitations in this respect. By comparison with the major government action proposed by the Senate committee, former Industry
Minister Pepin spoke in 1972 of a modest role of "influence,"
not a master plan.[61] On balance that modest role would seem
the practical one for government in Canada, and it would not
seem reasonable to expect any revolutionary change in managerial behavior to be inspired by such a role.

Results of the Industrial Strategy Review

In the early stages of the current surge of interest in industrial strategy many people expected some clear statements of
policy by the government on the major subjects examined in
this chapter. Some writers encouraged that expectation by setting forth relatively precise guidelines for industrial strategy.[62]
Government assurances that an industrial strategy would be announced by fall 1972 did more to feed the expectation. By late
1972, however, it was readily apparent to informed people that
such an outcome was entirely unrealistic. Only very limited
definition of policies was likely immediately, and modest further
definition would come only over an extended period. To understand this prospect, one must visualize the dimensions of the
review process.

For several years there had been discussions of industrial
strategy within the Department of Industry, Trade and Commerce. The work was limited to manufacturing and tended to
focus on the problems of individual industries, one at a time.
Furthermore, the approach, as one Canadian put it to me, was
"largely limited to just patching up weak industries" without
considering their basic status within the important international

economic constraints of Canada's position.

The need for a much broader approach to the question was doubtless stirring in the minds of some people throughout this period. But it received strong impetus from two widely publicized reports in late fall 1971, first the Science Council study *Innovation in a Cold Climate*,[63] and then the leaked version of the Gray Report published in *Canadian Forum* magazine.[64] The former made a strong case for the need for an industrial strategy as a basis for a healthy economy. The latter added a major increment of importance to the concept by emphasizing that the varied aspects of a policy on foreign investment could not be soundly determined without reference to a general strategy for all investment. By the end of 1971 the need had apparently achieved universal acceptance throughout the government, among all political parties, and out across the breadth of the land—a quite extraordinary kindling of nationwide interest.

This massive interest promptly led to the next act of the play —an equally broad study process set in motion during 1972. The center was a relatively small unit in the Department of Industry, Trade and Commerce charged with responsibility for directing the study of industrial strategy. The new dimensions of the concept were evident in its broad approach to the work, encompassing all the varied subjects discussed here. Consistent with this broadened concept, the unit was working closely with people in external affairs, finance, labor, and other departments. But the activities of this small group were a minute part of the total national effort being devoted to developing industrial strategy ideas and plans. It appeared that every subunit in the government with any conceivable interest in the subject was making studies and putting forward ideas which it hoped would achieve blessing under the apparently magic power of industrial strategy. Furthermore, the process had spread throughout the private sector, with all manner of business associations, labor groups, and the like also developing plans to present to the government.

With this picture in mind, one has no difficulty in appreciating why expectations of concrete statements of industrial strategy must be modest. The sheer time required to bring together the results of such a massive planning process must be measured in many months, even years. But more important, it is self-evi-

dent that a great deal of cutting and compromising among proposals will be required, and this will be extremely difficult both
because of the analytical problems of determining optimum
strategies on numerous issues such as have been analyzed here
and because of the characteristics of the Canadian national
decision-making process. It is because the difficulties along
these lines appear so immense that knowledgeable Canadians
had concluded that the enunciation of *a* single industrial strategy or even something close to it was utterly impossible.

What, then, might be expected from the study process? That
question has to be answered in two quite different dimensions:
(1) changes in the decision-making system and (2) redirection
of government policies. The former may ultimately be the more
profound effect. The massive study process has stirred a multitude of people to think hard about industrial strategy, and the
breadth of the goals guiding the current analyses has opened
their eyes to the wide dimensions of the subject. To be sure, the
outlook of many an individual official may have been lifted only
a little above his particular compartmentalized area. To some
degree the effort to advocate schemes which favor the interests
of his compartment of the economy may even have reinforced
his commitment to that area.

But the exercise of analyzing the goals of the individual compartment with reference to broad national goals and of debating
them with people with different sets of subgoals will surely
have a strong educational impact on the whole decision-making
system. If, as expected, the discussion of industrial strategy
continues for several years, a multitude of officials will become
accustomed to this sort of perspective, and that will certainly
carry over into the handling of their regular responsibilities.
Thus the effect of the industrial strategy study process may appear in a subtle, not readily measured, but profound change in
the way in which people throughout the bureaucracy and leadership function in the ongoing decision-making process on
many fronts. It should be noted that the modest tangible results
from the many proposals now being generated may frustrate
some people and produce some negative backlash against the
idea of industrial strategy planning, but some of the underlying
change in broader outlooks will surely be retained.

This subtle change in the decision-making process will prob-

ably be matched by a not much better defined redirection of
government policies. Given the divergence of both conceptual
views and concrete plans, arriving at a publicly enunciated industrial strategy is certainly impossible. However, it is equally
clear that action, or often inaction, on many matters affecting
industrial strategy must be taken by the government. At the
policy-making levels of government, the present study process
is defining strategy issues, and key people are formulating their
personal priorities and philosophies.

The blend of their approaches will be the key to the redirection of government policy. Its substance will appear gradually,
perhaps in a few basic policy statements, but more importantly
in the handling of major issues as they arise. It seems likely that
the decisions taken will often appear to be based on different
industrial strategy approaches, a characteristic upon which the
political opposition will harp. But this will be due to a sense
among government leaders that clear policy decisions on some
of the types of issues discussed above are not wise.

Indeed, the central cabinet figure in the 1972 debates, Jean-
Luc Pepin, was widely quoted in Ottawa as saying that there
would be no single industrial strategy but rather a number of
strategies. To many critics of the government, this outcome may
appear to be no real change from the past. However, that would
not seem a realistic appraisal. In practical terms, there is likely
to be a real change in that, to a modest degree in one area after
another, one will find greater emphasis on certain basic strategy
concepts like rationalization and product niches.

Recognizing that policy and decision-making changes in
Canada are inevitably evolutionary rather than revolutionary,
one must note that the emergence of guiding concepts was already under way before the present studies began. The effect of
the present massive study process, therefore, will presumably be
simply to accelerate the formulation of the concepts in decision-
making centers (individuals and groups) and to provide a
public visibility pressure for their application. The present discussion has created public awareness of the concepts, which
assures that their relevance will be constantly raised in public
comment on the handling of individual decisions, a fact that
politically sensitive decision makers will not ignore. Thus in the
future, both out of their own concern and in response to public

expectations, the policymakers will in practical terms be applying industrial strategy guidelines even though a strategy or even several strategies have not been explicitly set forth.

Notes

1. *The New Environment for Canadian-American Relations* (Montreal and Washington: Canadian-American Committee, 1972), p. 58.
2. Toronto *Daily Star,* December 23, 1971.
3. Calgary *Herald,* March 14, 1972.
4. Toronto *Daily Star,* August 30, 1972.
5. House of Commons *Debates,* May 15, 1972, p. 2,278.
6. *The New Environment,* p. 17.
7. Toronto *Globe and Mail,* February 21, 1972.
8. Toronto *Daily Star,* September 19, 1972.
9. House of Commons *Debates,* December 9, 1971, p. 10,336.
10. Toronto *Globe and Mail,* November 20, 1971.
11. *A Science Policy for Canada,* Report of the Special Senate Committee on Science Policy (Ottawa: Government of Canada, 1972); and *Innovation in a Cold Climate* (Ottawa: Science Council of Canada, Report #15, 1971).
12. Maurice Lamontagne, "The Sickness of Canadian Industry," *Canadian Forum,* June 1972, p. 20.
13. *Innovation in a Cold Climate,* p. 45.
14. *Ibid.,* p. 39.
15. House of Commons *Debates,* November 18, 1971, p. 9,688.
16. *Foreign Direct Investment in Canada* (Ottawa: Government of Canada, 1972), p. 6.
17. Toronto *Globe and Mail,* March 31, 1972.
18. A. E. Safarian, *Foreign Ownership of Canadian Industry* (Toronto: McGraw-Hill, 1966), pp. 280–86; and N. H. Lithwick, *Canada's Science Policy and the Economy* (Toronto: Methuen, 1969), pp. 82–83.
19. Arthur J. Cordell, *The Multinational Firm, Foreign Direct Investment, and Canadian Science Policy* (Ottawa: Science Council of Canada, Special Study #22, December 1971), pp. 43–46.
20. Lamontagne, *op. cit.,* p. 20.
21. *Eleventh Report of the Standing Committee on External Affairs*

and National Defense Respecting Canada-U.S. Relations, Second Session, Twenty-eighth Parliament (Ottawa: Government of Canada, 1970), p. 31.

22. House of Commons *Debates,* March 9, 1972, p. 671.
23. Toronto *Globe and Mail,* February 3, 1973.
24. Toronto *Daily Star,* May 11, 1972.
25. Cordell, *op. cit.,* p. 44.
26. Toronto *Daily Star,* May 19, 1972.
27. Toronto *Daily Star,* July 13, 1972.
28. Toronto *Daily Star,* October 20, 1971.
29. *Innovation,* p. 30.
30. Robert L. Perry, *Galt, U.S.A.* (Toronto: The Financial Post, 1971), pp. 54–61.
31. *Innovation,* p. 30.
32. House of Commons *Debates,* December 29, 1971, p. 10,809.
33. Toronto *Globe and Mail,* November 17, 1971.
34. John Fayerweather, "The Mercantile Bank Affair," *Columbia Journal of World Business,* November–December 1971, p. 41.
35. *The Problems and Potentials of Canadian Manufacturing* (Ottawa: The Conference Board, Canadian Studies No. 24, 1972), pp. 98–100.
36. *Ibid.,* p. 30.
37. Toronto *Daily Star,* January 10, 1972.
38. House of Commons *Debates,* March 21, 1972, p. 1,037.
39. Staff Studies, Economic Council of Canada, Ottawa: Information Canada: #21, D. J. Daly, B. A. Keys, and E. J. Spence, *Scale and Specialization in Canadian Manufacturing;* #23, D. Walters, *Canadian Income Levels and Growth: An International Perspective;* #31, H. H. Postner, *An Analysis of Canadian Manufacturing Productivity;* and E. C. West, *Canada-United States Price and Productivity Differences in Manufacturing Industries,* 1963.
40. *Eleventh Report* [note 21], pp. 18–20.
41. I. A. Litvak, C. J. Maule, and R. D. Robinson, *Dual Loyalty* (Toronto: McGraw-Hill, 1971), p. 62.
42. An analysis of the auto price situation was presented in the House of Commons by former Industry Minister Pepin: "In 1965, when the agreement was signed, the average weighted price differential between Canadian and U.S. cars was over 8 per cent at . . . the 92.5 per cent [exchange] rate. As the benefits of the agreement gradually bore fruit, the average price gap grew narrower until by 1970 the differential was down to 3.5 per cent. By 1971 it would have been 3 per cent, and for the

current model year about 2 per cent, had the value of the Canadian dollar remained unchanged." Pepin said that at the current exchange rate, the 1965 differential would have been 16 per cent, falling to 8 per cent for the 1972 models. The differential tended to be greater on more expensive cars, and on one subcompact the Canadian price before taxes was actually $61 less than in the United States. He listed the following factors as contributing to higher Canadian costs: transportation to dealers, sales tax on materials, higher cost of borrowed capital, greater overhead and administrative costs related to Canada's economy, and the burden of colder winters. House of Commons *Debates,* May 11, 1972, p. 2,192.

43. House of Commons *Debates,* February 24, 1972, p. 204.
44. Michael G. Duerr, *Tax Allocations and International Business* (New York: The Conference Board, 1972).
45. House of Commons *Debates,* March 2, 1972, p. 461.
46. Toronto *Globe and Mail,* May 4, 1972.
47. *The New Environment,* p. 15.
48. October 25, 1972.
49. Toronto *Globe and Mail,* February 23, 1972.
50. "Canada-U.S. Relations," *International Perspectives,* Autumn 1972, p. 18.
51. Toronto *Daily Star,* September 19, 1972.
52. "Canada-U.S. Relations," p. 17.
53. House of Commons *Debates,* November 4, 1971, p. 9,330.
54. Toronto *Globe and Mail,* August 22, 1972.
55. *The New Environment,* p. 22.
56. Lamontagne, *op. cit.,* p. 18. Reproduced by permission of the *Canadian Forum.*
57. *Ibid.,* p. 20.
58. John H. McArthur and Bruce R. Scott, *Industrial Planning in France* (Boston: Harvard Business School, 1969).
59. Toronto *Globe and Mail,* May 24, 1972.
60. *Business Week,* May 27, 1972, p. 32.
61. Toronto *Daily Star,* April 11, 1972.
62. For example, the series of articles on "An Industrial Strategy for Canada" in *Canadian Forum,* January–February 1972.
63. *Innovation.*
64. "A Citizen's Guide to the Herb Gray Report," *Canadian Forum,* December 1971.

5 National policy on foreign investment

W̲ E COME NOW, at last, to the central subject of this analysis: Canadian national policy on foreign investment, around which converge the elements of attitudes, national decision making, and industrial strategy already discussed. The net effect of these influences to date has been a large amount of study resulting in substantial published output, including five recent official and semi-official reports, the Gray Report prepared for the Trudeau cabinet, the Wahn Report by a House of Commons committee, official Ontario reports by a select committee of the Parliament and an interdepartmental task force, and a study on multinational corporations by the Science Council.[1] But the nature and number of specific actions taken have been quite moderate. This chapter will look at the objectives and obstacles influencing present trends in policy and then consider the directions in which Canada seems to be moving in handling the foreign investment question.

Objectives and Obstacles

The following paragraph from the Gray Report provides the best available statement of the national consensus on goals for a policy on foreign investment:

In examining the impact of foreign direct investment on Canada's political, economic and social development, three key issues emerge. The first relates to the kind of economy and environment in which Canadians want to live and work. Can the Canadian people and their governments develop the sort of stimulating and innovative environment that will result in a less truncated and less marginal economy? Can they develop the kind of economy that will help to keep creative Canadians in Canada and to reduce the present heavy reliance on the ideas and technology of others? The second is whether our economic structures, institutions, and policies provide the necessary tools for Canada to control and direct its national priorities. The third is the distribution of the costs and benefits from foreign direct investment between Canada, the foreign investor, and the foreign investor's own economy.[2]

These words summarize concisely the interests expressed in the previous chapters, essentially the quest for national identity, control of national affairs, and optimum benefits from foreign investment.

The assortment of policies which have emerged as means to achieve these goals represent the governmental efforts to respond to pressures for action while limited by a variety of constraints. The pressures for action are quite visible and straightforward. First, as we have noted in Chapter 2, there is substantial public opinion with a nationalistic orientation which, from a purely political point of view, requires that the government move in this direction. Second, there are a variety of areas of action in which government officials see possibilities of concrete gains for Canada both by increasing economic benefits and by decreasing the vulnerability of Canada, especially vis-à-vis the effects of U.S. economic policy.

The deterrents on policy actions are of a more subtle nature, but they are very strong. First, Canadians are understandably cautious about any disruption of their basic economic system. Regardless of whatever shortcomings may be attributed to the extent of foreign control, the fact is that an economy incorporating a very large degree of foreign ownership has functioned quite well for Canada. Because the foreign control component is so large, any government that fiddles with the mechanism might risk substantial impairment to the whole functioning of the economy.

At least two risks or types of damage are recognized by Canadians. The most obvious is that a significant change in foreign investment policy might be interpreted among multinational firms as a sign that Canada was becoming a less favorable climate in which to operate, and the rate of expansion of their activities there might decline. While Canadians are currently quite confident of their ability to cover the financial requirements of new investment, they are most anxious to continue the growth of activities of multinational firms which contribute to job creation and the steady inflow of technological and managerial skills. The second concern lies in the possible effects of policy actions on the operating systems of multinational firms. It is difficult to predict the effects of any specific policy proposal aimed at influencing, for example, the R&D or export policies of a multinational firm. The internal system of the firm has sufficient interrelationships among functions so that a policy affecting any one function may have assorted other effects which might work to the disadvantage of Canadians.

A second, closely related deterrent lies in the general complexity of this whole subject in terms of Canadian interests and effects on the Canadian economy and society. This comes through very clearly in the intimate picture of the role of foreign investment in the affairs of a single Canadian city presented in *Galt, U.S.A.*[3] Through a series of intimate descriptions of the lives of people, one can see that whether foreign ownership is good or bad depends very much on an individual's particular needs and personality. For some managers working in a foreign firm it is highly desirable and for some it poses special problems, and the same types of differences apply to labor leaders, workers, and others.

By the same token, the complex interaction of benefits and disadvantages in the R&D, financing, export capability, and other characteristics of foreign-firm activity is extremely hard to unravel. Policymakers are handicapped by the lack of thorough knowledge of the economic effects of foreign investment. On the basis of the most penetrating study of the multinational firm yet undertaken, Raymond Vernon was able to conclude only that his findings "suggest . . . that the impact of international investment is not necessarily measured by such figures as yield on investment, payments to labor, and tax payments. The effects recorded by these measures could be swamped by those outside the recording net, especially if the effects run over a number of years."[4] The Gray Report, as previously quoted, accepts the general conclusion of prior studies that foreign investment is economically beneficial, but in emphasizing that the studies "involve numerous qualifications," it highlights their incompleteness.[5] Carl Beigie, formerly of the Private Planning Association, observes: "The Gray Report is a disappointment for what it failed to include . . . the report has added little to our knowledge concerning such basic and still unresolved questions as the overall impact of foreign direct investment on Canadian growth, employment, prices, product diversity, and the balance of payments."[6]

While some government officials responsible for performance in a particular segment of the economy may see merit in policy actions specifically directed toward it, as one moves higher up the governing structure to men with a broad responsibility, lack of knowledge of overall impact and the complexities of side effects of policy action in a particular area become of greater concern and therefore a substantial deterrent to policy action. Premier William Davis of Ontario has stated this philosophy of caution concisely: "To threaten precipitate action [on foreign investment] at this time is to gamble with the livelihood of countless Canadians."[7]

A third deterrent, closely related to the second, is the diversity of interests in Canada and their relevance in the national decision-making process described in Chapter 3. The basic conclusion of that chapter was that the combination of traditionally moderate government action and the problems of government-business and Ottawa-provincial relations result in a slow-moving and mild decision-making process. Federal concern on this count was demonstrated in the handling of the takeovers bill in 1972, both in the initial exclusion of the provinces from the review process to simplify administration and then in the acceptance of an obligation to consult them as a result of pressure during the Commons debate. The great variety of differences in attitudes and complexities of problems which we have reviewed thus far adds up to a situation in which the characteristic Canadian decision-making process can only be expected to move very slowly and very tentatively.

The fourth deterrent is of a basic philosophical nature. Canadians are inhibited from taking any substantial measures which would impair the operations of the large body of existing foreign investment by their fundamental commitment to private property rights and to fairness in general. There have been three significant cases which illustrate this deterrent. The first was legislation enacted in 1964 to encourage Canadian magazines, which would have made the cost of advertising purchased from foreign-controlled publications ineligible for tax deduction purposes. This would have roughly doubled the cost for Canadian firms of advertising placed in *Reader's Digest* and *Time,* the only publications falling in this category, thereby seriously impairing their profitability. The act, when ultimately passed, exempted these publications so that the provisions would only have the effect of preventing future development of foreign-controlled publications and protecting Canada from a further incursion of U.S. publishing interests. Walter Gordon, Minister of Finance at that time, has said that the exception was made because of U.S. pressure as the *quid pro quo* for U.S. acceptance of the Auto Pact.[8] While this pressure was doubtless a factor, it is also true that the publications had a strong following for their case and that the Canadian sense of fair treatment provided significant support for the exception.

The second case was the treatment of the Mercantile Bank, a subsidiary of the First National City Bank of New York, the only foreign-controlled bank in Canada.[9] In this case the government did include in the Bank Act of 1967 a provision which sharply limited the growth of Mercantile and ultimately forced it into a plan to sell 75 percent of its stock to Canadians. This provision was strongly criticized at the time by many Canadians as unfair, and it is quite likely that it could not have been accomplished but for an unusual combination of circumstances involving the determined efforts of Walter Gordon in the cabinet and inept handling by the bank which led to substantial adverse public reaction. The third case was the 1971 effort to force Merrill Lynch and other foreign investment firms already established in Ontario to reduce their ownership or otherwise limit their activities. Canadians did not go along with this proposal despite very strong urgings on the part of the investment community.

Overall, therefore, it is fairly clear that Canadians are not prepared to take the types of forceful adverse actions against established foreign-owned firms which are experienced in many less developed countries. The policies Canada adopts affecting existing firms may be expected to fall in the relatively narrow range of restraints which do not substantially limit business freedom and ability to make profitable use of private property.

Policies and Actions

The events of the past year or so provide a good picture of the patterns of policies and actions which are evolving out of these objectives, pressures, and deterrents.

At the federal level, the notable events were the publication of the Gray Report and the proposed investment review bill. But there were other events, particularly in tax legislation and aspects of the emerging industrial strategy, which also fall within the area of foreign investment policy. At the provincial level during 1972, legislation was proposed in Ontario requiring that all foreign companies have a majority of Canadians on the board of directors by October 1973, and the government decided, at least temporarily, to stop making forgivable loans to foreign companies in the program to help depressed areas. Ontario also closed the book distribution field to further entry by foreign firms, restricted their role in periodical distribution, and required 75 percent Canadian ownership for all future foreign entries in the investment business. New legislation has been proposed by both Ottawa and Ontario to foster Canadian book publishing. Manitoba and Quebec are restricting entry by investment firms in much the same way as Ontario. While Alberta's effort, described in Chapter 3, to increase taxation of resource firms is industry-wide, in fact it may be interpreted as part of the foreign investment area since such a large portion of the firms are foreign-controlled. The new British Columbia government is reported to be planning to require that all new mining companies be 51 percent Canadian-owned.

While each of these events has its individual significance, it is their relevance in the total pattern which is most interesting in looking to the future. Just as it seems unlikely that there will be a clearly enunciated industrial strategy, it is improbable that there will be a well-defined, official policy on foreign investment. The Gray Report experience is ample evidence on that point. Long anticipated as an official declaration of policy, the report ultimately appeared as something different—a task force staff document with an aura of government blessing. It recommended screening of all new foreign investment. The government then proposed screening only of takeovers, and Trudeau firmly stated that there was no intention in the foreseeable future to extend screening to other investments. Then, in early 1973, he proposed moving to precisely that goal. The unmistakable implication was that Gray, perhaps with the support of other cabinet members, had recommended the policy in the report and had been voted down by the majority of the cabinet. Subsequently, after his sharp election shock, Trudeau proposed moving toward the Gray Report goal.

While the position of the Trudeau cabinet is the official policy of the moment, that technicality is not very helpful for those contemplating the future, especially in light of the very shaky political prospects of the Liberal government. It is more useful, therefore, to think of national policy in terms of directions of emerging national consensus which are likely to guide government decisions within the range of political contexts that may be expected for the next few years. Taking this view, one can discern certain patterns which may be grouped under six headings: benefits-control-ownership; indirect influences on behavior; development of Canadian-owned industry; key sectors; extraterritorial legal issues; and multinational control.

BENEFITS-CONTROL-OWNERSHIP

One of the very striking developments in Canadian thinking has been the change in approach on the question of control. In earlier years the nationalistic pressures were predominantly directed at acquiring a greater degree of ownership of companies controlled by foreign firms. This objective was officially adopted for a brief period in Walter Gordon's 1963 budget, with the enactment of mild tax advantages favoring firms with 25 percent Canadian participation. The goal has subsequently been pursued only to the extent of encouragement in the Winters Guidelines that foreign firms offer stock to Canadians though to many people it remains a prime objective. The Wahn Report, for example, strongly endorsed measures to repatriate ownership of a large portion of many Canadian subsidiaries.

The Gray Report, however, is notable for its endorsement of a quite different concept on the control question. Like many other statements, the report indicates the financial impracticality of repatriating any substantial degree of ownership of foreign-controlled firms. But more important, it stresses repeatedly that in key matters such as research and development, exports, and the like, ownership is not a determining factor in control. For example, in industries where the cost of developing technology is high, a fully Canadian-owned firm is just as likely to be "truncated" as a foreign-owned company because the economics of competition lead it naturally to buy technology, not develop its own R&D. Indeed, the close ties of multinational firms with their parents often lead them to allocate some R&D to subsidiaries, which they would not do with licensees. So far as control is concerned, even minority-owned firms or licensees retain close ties with foreign firms to obtain help in the application of technological and managerial skills, and these ties carry with them important controls, for example, over exports, which dominant Canadian ownership cannot overcome. Thus the basic philosophy of the Gray Report is to essentially ignore the question of ownership and to concentrate on direct control or influence in those aspects of operations which are significant to Canada. The point of view of Canadians may variously be pressed through legislation, regulations, incentives, or direct bargaining.

New Directions. Underlying this approach are two basic concepts which may be the most important elements of national policy at this time: primary attention to maximizing economic benefits for Canada and a selective approach to control. The emphasis on economic results is prominent in recent official activity. The Gray Report starts its justification of the review process on this note, arguing that it will have both minimum negative economic effects and potentials for benefits. "Use of a new policy, the review process, which is cost-free will not result in any reduction in growth rate, and therefore will not be the cause of any reduction in per capita income or employment. On the contrary . . . the major function would be to negotiate . . . with a view to increasing the level of efficient economic activity and improving Canada's industrial structure. . . ."[10]

It is interesting to note that maximization of benefits, not control, is the prime interest of Joel Bell, the chief staffman for the Gray Report.[11] Throughout the 1972 discussions of the take-overs bill, the then Industry Minister Pepin and other government officials emphasized that the objective was not to limit foreign investment but to seek greater benefits for Canada from it. The emphasis on benefits is clear in the first sentence of Pepin's speech for the bill in Commons: "The objective . . . is to ensure that foreign takeovers of Canadian corporations take place only when such takeovers will bring appreciable benefits to Canada."[12]

This primary interest in benefits is not a new element in Canadian national policy on foreign investment. It has been the controlling factor in the very limited general government action up to the present. As was noted in Chapter 2, the majority of Canadians have been impressed with the perceived economic benefits of foreign investment and have been unwilling to take actions which might endanger those benefits. The strong nationalists, with their emphasis on repatriating ownership, have been the ones willing to give secondary emphasis to maximizing economic benefits.

The new development is the convergence of these two forces. The nationalistic drive has gained enough breadth and depth so that official policy actions have moved into the area where they must necessarily deal with the benefits-control-ownership mix. The important point in looking to the future is the evidence that the former dominance of the benefit criteria has prevailed. Thus, while the desire for greater control of national affairs is great in Canada, as we observed in Chapter 2, it appears that in the final crunch of formulating policies and actions with a broad impact, the economic benefits to Canada will probably be the controlling factor.

The selective approach to control is not new either, but it has emerged as a quite new factor in the Canadian scene. Its importance stems in considerable part from its advocacy by Professor Abraham Rotstein, the intellectual leader of the Committee for an Independent Canada. The concept was set forth by him in a CIC-sponsored book in 1972.[13] Rotstein starts with the theory of functional socialism of the Swedish economist Adler-Karlsson: "It is essentially a theory which separates *title* to property from the *functions* or powers of this property."[14] The latter include a large cluster of rights such as setting prices, building factories, determining working conditions, etc. The functional socialism concept shifts the direction of socialism from total control through public ownership of the title of property to control exercised selectively over the various functions of property. Basically, of course, this is the way our industrial society has evolved, with public control limiting the free exercise of individual aspects of private industry rights in a number of specific functions—advertising, child labor, pollution, etc.

But this lack of full novelty should not detract from the significance of the current emergence of this concept in the midst of the strong nationalists in Canada. What it does is to provide for this group a viable alternative to the prior preoccupation with achieving control through the ownership route. An immediate major change in direction is unlikely among the nationalists, for the ownership approach has a tradition and strong advocates. Thus the policy of advocating sale of a controlling interest in foreign firms to Canadians was clearly endorsed at the CIC meeting in Edmonton in September 1972, while the selective control concept did not appear as a formal proposal (in part, presumably, because it would be difficult to phrase, being more of a philosophy than an action approach). But the important thing is that the alternative is well planted among the strong nationalists, and because it is so much more practical than the ownership route, it is likely to govern the type of specific points to which they direct their efforts.

From this analysis, one may project with some confidence that the combination of primary attention to benefits and the selective control approach will dominate national policy. Thus, in all probability there will be no significant effort to pressure foreign subsidiaries in general to share ownership with Canadians. Confirmation for this expectation can be found in the relative mildness of the CIC policy on this point adopted at Edmonton in 1972, which said only that "the government should *state that it expects*" [emphasis added] sale of stock by subsidiaries rather than advocating pressures or compulsion.[15] If that is as far as the CIC will go, the main body of moderate Canadian nationalists will surely go no further on general ownership policy than the mild persuasion of the Winters Guidelines.

Major Applications. The substantive thrust of national policy may be expected to be toward the selective approach to optimizing benefits in the investment review process and interactions with subsidiaries. How far and in what directions the government will go in these areas is difficult to discern at this point, but some meaningful speculation is possible. Almost certainly the Foreign Investment Review bill will be enacted in 1973 unless the Trudeau government falls quickly and an early election is required. A Gallup poll reported that 69 percent of the population favored review with only 15 percent opposed and 16 percent with no opinion.[16] All parties support the general concept.

The initial step, the takeover review process, is a modest one which merely extends and formalizes the government intervention in major takeovers already undertaken on an ad hoc basis in the Dennison Mines (1970) and Home Oil (1971) cases. Annual takeovers probably affect less than 1 percent of the foreign-controlled business sector in Canada. From 1966 to 1969 they totaled $450 million, about one-eighth of capital inflow.

The element added in the 1973 bill—screening of new investments by companies not already established in Canada and of new businesses opened in unrelated lines by existing foreign-controlled firms—appears substantial, but quantitatively it will also have a modest impact. The most recent official data record some 8,700 foreign-controlled enterprises in Canada in 1967.[17] This magnitude and general observation suggest that the great majority of large to medium-sized international firms are already established there. Data for 1964 through 1967 show that new enterprises have ranged from 300 to 700 per year. No information is available about the nature of these additions, but general knowledge suggests that many are new incorporations by existing firms (e.g., a new sales or finance subsidiary) which would not be covered by the screening. The new coverage, then, will probably be limited in the main to smaller firms with just a few medium to large multinational firms entering each year. Likewise, a significant number of new enterprises by established firms going into new lines of business is unlikely. In the nature of modern business the greater portion of such moves are via the acquisition route already covered by the takeover proposal. Other than being an impediment to a number of smaller firms newly entering foreign operations in Canada, the chief utility of the proposal would therefore seem to be to meet a substantive objection to the 1972 takeovers bill. The objection was that by impeding takeovers, the government would be encouraging foreign firms to set up new businesses. The result would be to aggravate Canada's problem of too many companies for too small a market. A new foreign entry would become a competitor for the firm it might have taken over, perhaps driving it out of business, whereas the takeover would at least have given the owner a comfortable sellout price. Under the new provisions, the new business option would be subject to the same review process as the takeover, so it would not be a means to escape the net if the takeover were blocked.

The key questions are how fast and how much further the government will move. The proposed bill provides that the new investment review process will commence at a date to be determined by the government. Industry Minister Gillespie has indicated that it would not start until experience has been acquired with the takeover review process. Guesses in Ottawa in early 1973 were that this would mean a year or more after the bill passed. But most important, even the proposed bill would not touch the largest growth factor in foreign investment—expansion of existing firms in their established line of business, which comprises about 80 percent of new investment.

Recent events and a look at the fundamental influences provide a fair indication of the prospects for the speed and extent of the extension of the review process. In 1972 Trudeau explicitly denied any intent to go beyond takeover review.[18] That assertion could be discounted as a political move to facilitate passage of the takeovers bill. On the other hand, in light of the various deterrents to foreign investment policy noted above, it seems quite likely that Trudeau saw it as a logical course for national policy. Any procedure which involves government review of every significant expansion of activities of foreign subsidiaries would meet with tremendous business resistance. It is quite possible that the bureaucratic delays and attempts at negotiating changes perceived as favorable to Canada would be highly disruptive to the general economic progress of the country. Thus it would be consistent with the nature of decision making and government activities to avoid this sort of major action, which might upset the general apple cart. The government is going to find it is hard even to assess the full effects of each takeover and new business in light of both the immediate implications for the firms and the broad effects of industrial consolidations on capital distribution, entrepreneurship, and other aspects of the economy.

Another strong reason for going slowly in extension beyond takeovers is that there is a major difference between them and new investments in provincial relations. A takeover usually involves only an existing facility while new investments entail decisions on location of new plants—the most important issue for job-hungry provincial politicians. Former Industry Minister Pepin set forth the reasoning on this point quite candidly in his presentation of the takeovers bill to Commons.

> The extension of the review process to other forms of foreign direct investment could slow down the creation of new industry, partly through reduced business confidence at home and abroad and partly through the disruptive effects such a major intervention could cause, resulting in fewer jobs being created.[19]

The modest incursion into new investments in the proposed bill will not create major problems of this sort. But experience with it will give Canadians enough of a taste of the realities of the varied interests which will have to be balanced to reaffirm the wisdom of going slowly in moving to review of all new investment.

In a speech prior to presentation of the new bill, Industry Minister Gillespie suggested an intermediate option which is more likely if and when the government feels the need to take another step, namely, registration of new investment. This is a new item on the agenda of discussion.[20] It would be a much less onerous burden for business and carry much less serious implications for the job-competition interests of the provinces. It would not in fact be much of a change in light of the advance information foreign firms already are giving the government in many cases because of requests for regional development aid, R&D grants, etc. It would have a moderate degree of real practical value for the government in giving it time to try to negotiate with companies to optimize the benefits of new investments for Canada, using limited bargaining levers rather than the absolute control of full screening, which is menacing and thus deterring to business. Thus one can visualize this step as a practical one within the range of attitudes and national decision-making capacity that would satisfy the bulk of moderate Canadian nationalists as a next step a few years from now.

Beyond the relatively well-defined question of investment review, one enters into a very broad area of potential government efforts to exert selective control in the ongoing operating functions of foreign-owned firms so as to optimize benefits for Canada. Much of this is, of course, already under way in fields like research and resource development, and the future approaches will be governed in large part by the questions discussed in our chapter on industrial strategy, this being one reason that subject is so central to foreign investment policy. The efforts quite likely will be broadened and strengthened gradually, and there will probably be some coordination of the process as the experience with the anticipated review agency develops. One possibility is some form of employment control. The Ontario Employment Standards Act of 1971 requires that notice be given to the government of plant shutdowns, and efforts are being made to extend this sort of intervention. Nationalists pressing this goal stress as supporting evidence that from June 1970 to June 1971, 76 foreign plants closed in Ontario, with 10,000 workers involved.[21]

Much of the effort in this respect will depend upon the experience with the Foreign Investment Review Agency to be established under the review bill. For many years nationalists have been advocating a central government unit with comprehensive responsibility over foreign investment. In fact, out of recent events a unit has been emerging in the Ministry of Industry, Trade and Commerce with this role, and the new bill will formalize and expand its functions. The future magnitude and success of both the review function and the other forms of control over foreign-controlled firms will be determined to a very large extent by the nature of the agency's relations with business and the provinces and its internal competence. In the industrial strategy chapter we cited several examples of Canada's difficulties in its government-business process—the STOL aircraft, the regional economic development program, etc. The magnitude and significance of government involvement in even a portion, let alone all, of the expansion of foreign-controlled business are far in excess of these activities. Thus, one can readily predict that the effective development of the Foreign Investment Review Agency will be a long and hard job, and how far it will be able to extend its activities beyond the specific review functions is quite uncertain at this juncture.

The Emerging Relationship. In concluding this section it is well to step back a little and look at the pattern of relationships bearing on control-benefits issues that has been evolving. The strong nationalists tend to think of the takeover review process and further steps as directed rather singlemindedly to reducing the degree of foreign investment in Canada. The officials involved would be firmly set in opposition to the foreign-owned firms, stoutly bargaining against them, perhaps even combative in their interactions.

This, however, has not been the reality to date, nor is it likely to be in the future. The reality of relations between Canadian officials and foreign-owned firms is a mixture of cooperation and bargaining underlain by a sense of basic mutuality of interests, with conflicts over operating specifics rather than fundamentals. This pattern obtains in the numerous interactions currently in process concerning research plans, new factories, and the like. There is every reason to presume that it would carry forward into new mechanisms like the takeover screening process. While there would undoubtedly be hard bargaining in them, as there is in current interactions, the essential characteristic would be further development of the collaborative relationship.

INDIRECT INFLUENCES ON BEHAVIOR

The investment review process and government communication on specific functional activities can be packaged under the overall heading of direct intervention with foreign-owned firms to further Canadian interests. The chief alternative strategy for pursuing the goal of maximizing benefits is to foster indirect influences which may push the firms in that direction. The Winters Guidelines were the first notable step in that direction. The other main approaches are financial disclosure requirements and Canadianization of management.

The idea of requiring a greater degree of financial disclosure by foreign-owned firms has been consistently advocated by Canadian nationalists. The objective in part is simply to provide more information to serve as a basis for determining policies. But most people perceive the reporting process as a means for exerting pressure on companies to perform in ways which are beneficial for Canada. The thought is that the need to report publicly on such functions as research and exports will result in greater management efforts to satisfy Canadian criteria of good performance. Since the mid-sixties the government has received on a confidential basis under the Corporations and Labour Union Returns Act (CALURA) basic data on all foreign-controlled firms (federal and provincial) as well as quarterly and annual reports from the larger foreign-owned subsidiaries—all designed to assess their performance under the Winters Guidelines. Data from both sources are summarized for public release. The federal government moved moderately further in this direction by requiring a limited degree of public financial reporting by larger federally incorporated firms under the 1970 Corporations Act amendments.

From all indications this is as far as the government is likely to go in the matter of mandatory financial disclosure. The Gray Report is notably silent on the subject. The widely recognized sticking point is the position of a number of privately owned Canadian firms strongly opposing any general measure that forces private enterprise to make financial data known to the general public. It is an interesting measure of the attitudes and values of the Canadian government that it is unwilling to adopt any mandatory financial disclosure policies which would clearly discriminate against foreign-owned firms. Thus the existing reporting process, which serves the essential needs of the government itself, is probably as far as it is willing to go.

The other significant avenue for greater indirect influence is the policy of increasing Canadian participation in the management of foreign-owned firms. Since virtually all the operating executives of subsidiaries are already Canadians, the main thrust of this approach is now directed at membership of boards of directors. The values of this approach are subject to serious dispute in Canada. Advocates of the step see a modest gain in the actual decision making of managements in Canada but a more important gain in the sensitizing of parent company executives to Canadian viewpoints by the representations to them from the Canadian directors.[22]

Political viewpoints on Canadianization of boards have composed a mixed picture. The Ontario government took the first concrete position with its decision to require a majority of Canadian directors by October 1973. After the 1972 election Robert Stanfield, leader of the Conservatives, in listing actions he would take if he became prime minister, noted such a measure as the only item on foreign investments. External Affairs Minister Sharp has characterized the requirement as "symbolic rather than of real significance."[23] The Gray Report concluded that "the benefits to be derived are likely to be modest,"[24] though Gray himself approved the Ontario initiative as a good step.[25] Early in 1973 the Trudeau government announced its intention to seek legislation for this purpose, apparently as a concession to the Conservative viewpoint. As a practical matter, most foreign-owned companies either already have Canadian directors or regard meeting the requirement as a minor problem. One gains the distinct impression, therefore, that its adoption at the federal level is of no great consequence.

DEVELOPMENT OF CANADIAN-OWNED INDUSTRY

While most Canadians generally accept as impractical the thought of repatriating ownership of any appreciable portion of present foreign investment, the national consensus does favor efforts to promote a steady shift toward a greater degree of Canadian ownership of industry by fostering national businesses. All political parties concur on this as a stated policy. Efforts already taken in that direction include some differential tax measures, establishment of the Canada Development Corporation, and the program to support industrial R&D.

The R&D situation illustrates the chief problem in achieving major accomplishments toward this goal. The government is regularly faced with the choice between using its resources to maximize overall industrial development or discriminating to help Canadian-owned firms. The R&D program has by and large been governed by the former criterion. Recognizing that a large portion of the capabilities for achievement of technology-based industrial progress lies with the foreign-owned firms, the government has allocated some 50 percent of R&D money to them. The same is essentially true of the large sums budgeted for development of depressed regions. The only substantial departure from this pattern was the 1972 decision of the Ontario government to limit its forgivable loans to Canadian-owned firms.

So long as financial support or other forms of encouragement are motivated by a desire to achieve progress for Canada as a whole, it would appear that governments cannot go too far in discriminating in favor of Canadian firms. In view of such major factors as the desire of the people for jobs and a higher standard of living and the moderate nationalist philosophy of the majority, it is likely that these limits on a nationalistic approach will not permit the discriminatory pattern of support programs to go far enough to have an appreciable general effect.

The other approach to differential support lies in general measures, especially provisions designed to give Canadian-owned firms a financial advantage. An example of this approach was the enactment in 1971 of a tax measure which favors Canadian firms in takeovers of small firms. A small Canadian firm pays only a 25 percent income tax compared to 40 percent for large firms. If a nonresident firm acquires a small firm, it must now retroactively pay the difference between the 40 percent and 25 percent rate for the years prior to the acquisition, but a Canadian firm does not have this obligation. To some degree, efforts in this field are simply directed at attempting to equalize tax effects which are currently disadvantageous to Canadian firms. For example, U.S. tax laws allow deduction of interest on loans used for takeovers, but Canadian laws had not allowed the same treatment until it was incorporated in the 1971 tax act.

One hears proposals in Canada to carry the discriminatory tax policy further. For example, James Gillies, former dean of the York University Business School, who won a Conservative seat in Parliament in the 1972 election, proposed during the campaign that there be different tax rates according to degree of Canadian ownership of firms.[26] The CIC has endorsed a proposal that foreign-controlled firms pay income taxes at the rate in the home country, which for U.S. firms would mean 48 percent vs. 40 percent for Canadian firms.

But one doubts if the discriminatory taxation approach will go much further than it already has in Canada. There is in the first instance the basic commitment to equity and fair play mentioned previously. On top of this is the highly practical value for Canada of preserving its reputation as having a favorable investment climate. Its image is currently somewhat tarnished by the combination of rising nationalism and uncertainty in domestic policies on labor, combines, and other matters. Adoption of a policy of discriminatory taxation would be a serious matter because, despite many nationalistic measures in other countries, this particular approach is not common.

All things considered, therefore, it would appear that the scope for efforts to build up Canadian-owned business vis-à-vis foreign-owned industry is quite limited. Consequently, despite strong desires among Canadians to move in this direction, actions will be limited to moderate discrimination in industrial support and tax policies along with some direct efforts like the CDC financing.

As a footnote to this section, mention should be made of recurring suggestions that Canada foster the development of Canadian-owned multinational firms as a counter to the influence of multinationals in Canada and as a means to strengthen the country's overall international economic role. Currently there are a few Canadian multinationals, notably Massey Ferguson, International Nickel and Alcan. Technically the latter two are foreign-owned because a little more than 50 percent of their stock is in foreign hands, but the ratio has shifted steadily toward Canadian control, with majority Canadian control expected soon.

Most people feel it is unlikely that any significant number of

Canadian firms could make the grade as new multinationals. There is even the possibility that Canada may lose ground in this respect. In 1972 Canadian tax laws on foreign income were made considerably less favorable than they had been. The president of Massey Ferguson said that this change might result in his company moving its headquarters to the United States.[27] As noted previously, the company's U.S. operations have been growing faster than those in Canada. It has also threatened that the drive for wage parity with the United States may push it in this direction.[28] While there may be a fair amount of talk for political effect in these views, they do convey the picture of an environment that is not likely to foster growth of multinational firms.

Ironically the current tax changes were instigated in part by arguments that Canadian multinational firms had an unfair advantage over strictly domestic firms because of lower effective tax rates—foreign income was not taxed until it was paid to stockholders of the parent firm.[29] In addition to hurting domestic competitors, this situation was said to be encouraging competitors to set up U.S. subsidiaries and possibly to move there. This would appear to be a "damned if you do and damned if you don't" situation, clearly not conducive to evolution of multinational firms based in Canada.

KEY SECTORS

By contrast with the relatively slow evolution and minor tenor of policies affecting foreign investment in general, Canadians have taken quite vigorous action on foreign participation in key sectors (see Chapter 1). There are now firm measures to limit foreign ownership in various aspects of the communications media and finance, including radio, television, magazine publication, book distribution, insurance, banking, and investment dealers. The further evolution of the key sector approach will depend in considerable part on the logics underlying it, so it is well to examine them briefly.

The rationale for this aspect of Canadian foreign investment policy is that particular elements of industry are of special importance to national identity, either in the preservation of Canadian culture, as in the case of communications media, or for the achievement of economic goals, as with banking. It is also clear, however, that the nature of the impact of foreign participation is an important consideration in these actions. The fields involved are ones in which contributions from foreign business are either small or may be acquired fairly readily without major direct ownership by foreign companies. The Canadian insurance industry, for example, is quite strong (one of the leading firms in the world is the Sun Life Company of Canada). Therefore the participation of foreign companies within Canada, aside from its competitive stimulus, is not particularly critical. In radio and television, foreign source programs are economically useful but they may be quite readily purchased without ownership involvement. These situations are notably different from such fields as the high-technology industries, in which close operating integration with foreign parent organizations is of major importance for the efficient transfer of skills to serve the Canadian economy, or for resource development, with its massive capital needs.

The related and somewhat confusing element in this picture has been the influence of competitive conditions. In all cases, and particularly in publishing and investment, the control has been designed to protect Canadian-owned business from greater incursions by foreign firms. While the preservation of indigenous business is defended on grounds of national interest, individual Canadian businessmen have clearly benefited in the process. The problem for Canadian policymakers has always been to sort out and balance the individual vs. the national interest, which requires an appraisal of the inputs of foreign participation and the cost of excluding or limiting it. While this may have been fairly easy in the early insurance and communications media cases, it appears to be increasingly difficult when the more complex and marginal situations are considered, as the Ontario investment house case demonstrates. Canadian firms argue that they are competent for Canada's needs and that the incursion of foreign firms is based in large part on their size and capital resources, which offer no special advantage for Canada. On the other hand, a reasonable argument can be made that the sophistication of the management skills of leading foreign firms is a major input in terms of Canada's desire to develop indigenous entrepreneurship. Then there is the even more complex question of the extent to which foreign firms are inclined to undertake investment on a minority basis and the degree of effort they will make in transmitting their managerial skills in such arrangements.

It is quite likely that the future will see a further extension of the key sector approach to foreign participation in Canadian business. However, the balancing of national and individual interests and the cost to Canada will be increasingly difficult to determine. This, along with the general change in philosophy downgrading the importance of ownership for control, is likely to result in a shift in the handling of these specific industries. One would expect greater emphasis to be put on direct controls or incentives to assure foreign inputs with maximum benefits for Canada. That approach will also avoid the ever-ticklish problem of dealing with existing foreign firms, which proved so troublesome in the *Reader's Digest/Time* and Mercantile Bank cases.

This pattern is already apparent in the efforts to strengthen the Canadian role in the publishing field. In 1972 only 5 percent of English-language books in Canada were published by Canadian-owned firms.[30] The portion of textbooks supplied to Canadian schools by Canadian firms had dropped from 40 percent in 1968 to about 20 percent in 1972. This situation aggravated the deep concern about the foreign impact on education created by the large number of foreign teachers in higher education. It was too late in this case to apply the ownership format to limiting foreign investment. So a program was generated to bolster the remaining contingent of Canadian publishers: Ontario made loans of almost $2 million to five Canadian firms to help them publish Canadian books and avoid their takeover by U.S. companies; the federal government allocated $500,000 to purchase Canadian books for libraries at home and abroad; the Canada Council doubled its grants for books authored by Canadians to $1 million; a $500,000 program was initiated to open book distribution offices in the United States; and other efforts were under way.

The approach to the publishing industry will not be duplicated exactly in other fields because its problems are in some respects unique. But the general concept would seem to fit the mood of Canada and the practicalities of other situations, so it will probably be part of the future national policy. The essence of the concept is a strong program to assure continued Canadian presence in each key sector, not just by restrictions but if necessary by positive steps such as the allocation of national resources for support.

EXTRATERRITORIAL LEGAL ISSUES

The question of extraterritorial application of foreign laws through foreign-controlled business apparently has minor actual effect on Canada, but it is a matter of high visibility and sensitivity in the country. There was a highly publicized incident in the late 1950s in which it was alleged that Ford of Canada was forced to refuse an order for vehicles from Communist China because of the U.S. Trading with the Enemy Law. There was also an incident in that period in which a U.S.-controlled financing firm refused to cooperate in a voluntary credit restraint program initiated by the Bank of Canada because it might involve violation of U.S. antitrust laws. Recently the issue flared up again when it was reported that a U.S.-owned firm had refused to sell a mini-submarine to the Russians because of U.S. government intervention. It has been said that the Canadian government itself had misgivings about a sale with such clear military implications. In any case, it purchased the submarine for domestic use.

Prospects of future difficulties from these two laws are quite limited. The governments worked out a procedure which assured that Canadian interests in trading-with-the-enemy cases would be protected by allowing U.S. subsidiaries to fill orders if no Canadian-owned firm could supply them. There is reasonably good collaboration between the governments on antitrust matters. However, the hazards of the extraterritorial impact of foreign government policies remain a high-priority subject in the national debate on foreign investment. The whole matter is regularly pushed to the fore by recognition of the degree to which Canada is vulnerable to effects of a great variety of U.S. government actions, ranging from its actions related to the balance of payments situation to product standards, wage controls and tax policies, because of the close integration with the U.S. economy in general and the massive participation of U.S. firms in Canadian industry. Specific aspects of extraterritoriality like the antitrust and trading-with-the-enemy matters are just the tip of a massive iceberg.

In this perspective the question of the relation of foreign government actions to Canadian interests becomes a major aspect of foreign investment policy. But it would not appear to be one in which the adoption of any specific measures applicable to foreign-controlled firms is likely to appear. Rather, the avenues for future progress lie more in closer cooperation with the U.S. government on a widening range of subjects. There are already more than a dozen joint Canada-U.S. boards. One may reasonably anticipate a growing volume of such communication between the governments and more formal institutions for joint handling of a variety of subjects—taxation, finance, etc. There is a clear Canadian interest in moving in this direction. The Wahn Report, for example, recommended: "In fields involving continuing co-operation with the United States . . . consideration should be given to the use of bilateral bodies where representatives of the two countries meet as equals."[31]

Progress in this direction, however, will inevitably be slow because of the traditional limits on the willingness of the U.S. government to modify its policies to fit Canadian interests and enter into limiting institutional commitments. The U.S. government has made certain major concessions to the Canadians, for example, exemption from large parts of the balance of payments program. Similarly, the Automotive Agreement represented an important concession for a special arrangement. But the history of these arrangements, which will be repeated in the future, is that each must be weighed very carefully on its merits and that progress is quite slow except in crisis situations.

MULTINATIONAL CONTROL

This discussion would not be complete without mention of Canadian interest in the concept of multinational control of multinational firms. External Affairs Minister Sharp has advocated some form of international regulation and Finance Minister Turner has spoken for an OECD code of conduct for multinational firms.[32]

At the moment, Canada is in a somewhat embarrassing position in the general field of multinational approaches to problems of international business because it has not collaborated in some key efforts already under way. Indeed John Crean, head of the Canadian Council of the International Chamber of Commerce, has spoken quite firmly of Canada's image as somewhat negative in the view of foreign officials because it has not signed the World Bank Convention on Investment Disputes or the OECD Investment Code, as well as being rather independent in exchange-rate and tariff actions.[33] There are good reasons for Canada's position in each of these matters. For example, with such a very large portion of its industry foreign-owned, Canada feels that the terms of the OECD code might become an untenable commitment, and the reason for special conditions on the Kennedy Round tariff reductions was noted in Chapter 4. However, while this reasoning is apparent to Canadians, it is not necessarily understood by other countries, and Canada's image as a collaborator in international arrangements suffers from its actions to some degree.

Still, there is logic in Canada's taking a leading part in exploring international arrangements to deal with host-nation concerns about multinational firms. Foreign investment is a bigger factor in its economy than in any other country, and in its general foreign policy Canada has sought the role of a leading mediator nation, standing between the largest countries and the many small ones. It is therefore quite possible that Canada will push initiatives in this direction. However, the road to international supervision is of course a long and hard one, so only modest real progress can be expected.

The Overall Tenor of Policy

Underlying the outlook for the main elements of foreign investment policy discussed above is the question of the overall tenor of the way in which they will be pursued. At the risk of oversimplification, I believe that the answer to this question will be determined by just a few key factors.

A major influence will be the mood of the country. The progression toward stronger policies in handling foreign-owned business has up to now been largely motivated by growing public pressure. My conclusion in Chapter 2 was that the continued growth of nationalistic pressure was uncertain but that it was a reasonable possibility. The other key point made in Chapter 2 was that the foreign investment issue rated relatively low in public opinion priorities. This ranking may fall yet lower. According to some political observers, one of the major results of the 1972 election was to elevate in importance the issue of national unity, since it demonstrated that the Trudeau approach had not only failed but perhaps had aggravated the English-French division among the populace. Employment and related economic issues are clearly in the forefront for reasons elaborated in Chapter 4. These economic and domestic unity issues are far more pressing and immediate in the eyes of most Canadians than foreign investment, especially as the latter is for the most part considered a positive economic contributor.

There is a great question mark here about the results of political instability on Canadian government action. In less developed countries a common ploy of insecure governmental leaders is anti-foreign-investment action. That possibility exists in Canada. Specifically, the Liberals, in an attempt to win over voters from the NDP, might adopt the CIC program. Lester Pearson pursued this strategy to a degree in backing Walter Gordon's foreign investment views when he had a minority government in the mid-1960s. But I doubt if any substantial shift of policy (as distinguished from political verbiage) is likely with this rationale. The Liberals lost more ground to the Conservatives than to the NDP, and in the long run the recovery of Liberal strength lies in maintaining a firm center position, not in swinging far to the left, though it might beneficially adopt a little of the NDP position, following the historical pattern described in Chapter 2.

The second factor is the growing conviction among a broad band of responsible Canadians that despite its generally beneficial character, foreign investment could be made to serve the national interests better. This is the maximizing-benefits psychology which pervades the Gray Report and current government thinking. It will provide a persisting momentum within the bureaucracy for continued movement in the types of specific policy areas discussed in the chapter on industrial strategy.

A third element is the increasing awareness among responsible people of the difficulty of assessing the costs and benefits of foreign investment and the great complexity of implementing general policies affecting it, deterrents discussed early in this chapter. The debate on the takeovers bill provided a vivid demonstration of this type of deterrent. A very large portion of the Commons committee examination of the bill was devoted to a multitude of side effects of the review system, ranging from major points like fostering creation of new firms by foreign investors frustrated in takeover bids to minor problems like the status of mortgages of insurance companies. The obvious point is that in a country in which most manufacturing is foreign-controlled, even measures of apparently simple and limited scope can have very diverse effects and risks. MP Marcel Lambert, the Conservative financial expert, described the problem aptly, if a little overdramatically, in commenting on the takeovers bill: "I think there is a great danger of creating a Frankenstein here."[34] The implications of such complexities, along with the limited knowledge of the overall effects of foreign investment, are clear. Responsible Canadian leaders are not likely to support substantial changes in policy affecting 60 percent of their manufacturing with such inadequate understanding of the consequences.

Fourth, and politically perhaps the most significant element, is the unabated quest of government leaders for new foreign investment, though with emphasis on decreasing the degree of dependence on U.S. sources. Just one item suffices to affirm this point. After running up an impressive record of actions relating to foreign investment in the spring of 1972, Premier Davis of Ontario spent much of August in Europe encouraging investors to come to his province.

Finally, there are the varied elements of the national decision-making process, discussed in Chapter 3, which militate against strong action by the federal government.

Putting these elements together, one can make some reasonably logical assumptions about the tenor of overall policy for the next few years. It seems inevitable that, as a political necessity, the federal and provincial governments must demonstrate that they are doing something about the foreign investment question. On the other hand, responsible behavior will restrain them from strong action. The outcome under these circumstances will probably be very much a continuation of the recent pattern, that is, a gradual pace of new actions which provide visible evidence to the public that foreign investment is receiving attention but which are cautious enough so that costs and risks are minimized and there is a fair assurance of some tangible benefit, either economically or for perceived national values—e.g., cultural identity—that fit the prevailing philosophy among officials. In the meantime, the whole foreign investment issue will be subordinated to the overriding need to strengthen the economy as a whole.

The program proposed by the minority Liberal government early in 1973 had these characteristics. The legislative plans set forth in the Speech from the Throne put major emphasis on measures to stimulate the economy and reduce unemployment.[35] The proposals bearing directly on foreign investment had a quite minor position, occupying a few lines:

Measures to ensure further control by Canadians over their economy by the screening of foreign takeovers of Canadian-owned business; measures respecting the transfer of technology from abroad and access to it by Canadian entrepreneurs; measures to increase Canadian participation in the ownership and control of resource projects; and, in consultation with the provinces, measures dealing with new direct foreign investment and the sale of land to foreigners. Measures that will restructure the Canada Corporations Act, including a requirement that a majority of the directors of federally-incorporated companies be Canadians.

The intent was further developed on January 10 by Alistair Gillespie, the new Minister of Industry, Trade and Commerce, in the speech cited above.[36]

The approach which I shall be proposing is as follows. First, the foreign takeover legislation. We will set up a review agency and gain some experience in the screening of takeovers. . . . The second and third aspects would follow. That is to say, that building on our experience and after consultation with the provinces, we will proceed with the registration and ultimately the screening of new investment. I would hope that the third aspect, the registration of licensing agreements affecting Canadian business, would follow promptly.

Then, on January 24, the Foreign Investment Review bill was introduced.

The logics of this program are readily perceived in the light of the analysis in this study, and therefore they provide a good guide to the outlook for foreign investment policies. The items in the Speech from the Throne are a viable compromise of interests. The introduction of the takeovers bill was inevitable. The second item, improved access to foreign technology, responds to the most universal and constructive element in Canadian thinking, that of building up Canadian-owned industrial capability. The board of directors provision is an obvious concession to the support the Conservatives had won on this point, pulling away from them one of the points they might have used in efforts to bring down the minority government. The efforts to increase Canadian ownership in resource projects provide an explicit concession to the NDP-CIC point of view, but they do not represent a radical step since this has already been the direction of government efforts, for example, in structuring the financing of the Arctic pipeline.

The most important element is the handling of the new investment question. The stated program implies a clear intent to ultimately achieve screening of all new investment. The limited probable outcome of proposed registration and screening was discussed earlier in this chapter. It is reasonable to assume that this limited result and the reasons for it were fully recognized by the Liberal government in their planning. One may fairly assess their proposal, therefore, as a masterful combination of practical goals, satisfactions for public opinion, and diffusion of responsibility. Registration, which is the likely long-term outcome, will be of some real value, with only minor detrimental effects. The stated goal of full screening gives comfort to the strong nationalists. However, the requirement of provincial consultation to achieve that goal makes substantial success either impossible or a distant prospect. For reasons which have been adequately explained already, the provinces are very unlikely to concede to Ottawa the right to yes-or-no decisions on new plants, and they will not take unto themselves this power for competitive reasons and because of the nationwide implications. One can readily predict, therefore, that there will be endless and probably fruitless consultation on that proposal. Meantime the relatively mild idea of registration can be enacted after suitable political discourse in a few years as a sequel to the takeover legislation and limited new investment review as a concrete response to nationalistic attitudes and to benefit optimization and planning.

Despite the apparent skillful political artistry in the legislative proposals, one must wonder if it may contain the seeds of some real difficulties not far down the road. We have here the type of risk I spoke of in Chapter 2 as inherent in the politics of nationalism. The Liberals have set forth a sequence of events which is sensible. But they have accelerated the legislative sequence by seeking immediate authorization for the partial new investment screening, even though its application is expected to be postponed a year or more. The reasoning is not given but it appears very much to be a political concession to the NDP, doubtless encouraged by Minister Gillespie, who is a member of the CIC. It would be entirely logical for the NDP and CIC to press the strategic advantage of the NDP power over Trudeau to put over as strong a piece of legislation as possible. It could be made palatable to more moderate nationalists by the promise of deferred application.

The question is whether the NDP and CIC will stop there and whether Trudeau, insecure not only against the other parties but within his own party, will feel able to resist if they do push for more. As I noted earlier, I believe the weight of influences is so heavily set in favor of moderation that it will prevail. But one cannot be sure. Canada has never experienced such a surge of nationalism with this type of political context. Thus, there is just a chance that stronger constraints on foreign investment will come faster, and that they will bring with them the risk of adverse economic consequences that the moderates fear.

Longer-Term Prospects

While uncertainties exist in this discussion of the immediate prospects for Canadian foreign investment policy, the longer-term prospects involve conflicting trends of basic elements whose resolution can scarcely be discerned. On the one hand, there has been a steady buildup of nationalistic reaction to foreign-controlled business which has created growing pressure for action by the government. So far the actions have been fairly limited in nature. Some people have observed that they are so minor that they simply postpone briefly the day when major actions must be taken; and indeed, in permitting the main body of foreign investment to grow in strength they contribute to magnifying the corrective steps which ultimately would have to be taken if the strongest nationalistic feelings seen today were to become widespread. Thus, if one were to project the current rate of growth of adverse reaction to foreign business, one would have to anticipate a substantially more restrictive government policy within a decade. Because of the uncertainties discussed earlier, one cannot project this trend with any assurance, but continuation of adverse reaction is a possibility that must be considered.

On the other hand, there are certain solid indicators of basic trends toward international integration and especially toward closer integration with the United States, ranging from George Grant's type of philosophical conclusion that Canada has already lost its identity as a nation, through the functionalist concepts of nonnationalists, to practical manifestations such as the continental rationalization of production and research in particular industries.

In a pragmatic free society, an evolutionary compromise between these two apparently opposing trends will undoubtedly be worked out in a reasonably satisfactory manner, though certainly with substantial tension and conflict. The exact form of the compromise, however, is hard to predict. My reading of past history and current influences leads me to expect that the main economic and government policy decisions will be governed by the second basic trend: the evolution toward integration. The attitudinal pressures for national identity would be satisfied to a large degree, as they are today, by measures which protect cultural and national identity, along with limited economic measures by which Canadian identity can be preserved with a minimum sacrifice to the standard of living. This expectation is based more on intuition than on logic, however; and, as in the past, it is probable that the actual course of events will be governed by forces that cannot be readily assessed at present.

Notes

1. *Foreign Direct Investment in Canada* (Ottawa: Government of Canada, 1972); *Eleventh Report of the Standing Committee on External Affairs and National Defense Respecting Canada-U.S. Relations,* Second Session, Twenty-eighth Parliament (Ottawa: Government of Canada, 1970); *Preliminary Report of the Select Committee on Economic and Cultural Nationalism, Second Session, Twenty-ninth Parliament* (Toronto: Government of Ontario, 1972); *Report of Ontario Interdepartmental Task Force* (Toronto: Government of Ontario, 1971); and Arthur J. Cordell, *The Multinational Firm, Foreign Direct Investment, and Canadian Science Policy* (Ottawa: Science Council of Canada, Special Study No. 22, 1971).

2. *Foreign Direct Investment in Canada, op. cit.,* p. 8.

3. Robert L. Perry, *Galt, U.S.A.* (Toronto: The Financial Post, 1971).

4. *Sovereignty at Bay* (New York: Basic Books, 1971), p. 187.

5. *Foreign Direct Investment, op. cit.,* p. 416.

6. "Foreign Investment in Canada," *Columbia Journal of World Business,* November–December 1972, p. 24.

7. Toronto *Daily Star,* January 22, 1972.

8. *A Choice for Canada* (Toronto: McClelland & Stewart, 1966).

9. John Fayerweather, "The Mercantile Bank Affair," *Columbia Journal of World Business,* November–December 1971, p. 41.

10. *Foreign Direct Investment,* pp. 451–52.

11. Toronto *Globe and Mail,* June 30, 1972.

12. House of Commons *Debates,* May 29, 1972, p. 2,631.

13. Abraham Rotstein and Gary Lax, eds., *Independence, The Canadian Challenge* (Toronto: Committee for an Independent Canada, 1972).

14. *Ibid.,* p. 79.

15. *Policy Resolutions* (Toronto: Committee for an Independent Canada, 1972), p. 2.

16. Toronto *Daily Star,* February 16, 1972.

17. *Canada's International Investment Position, 1926 to 1967* (Ottawa: Statistics Canada, 1971), p. 51.

18. Toronto *Daily Star,* May 20, 1972. See also Jean-Luc Pepin, Speech to Victoria (British Columbia) Chamber of Commerce, May 8, 1972, p. 13: "there is no 'second shoe' to be dropped after the next federal election."

19. House of Commons *Debates,* May 29, 1972, p. 2,362.
20. House of Commons *Debates,* January 10, 1973, p. 154.
21. Toronto *Daily Star,* March 28, 1972.
22. I. A. Litvak, C. J. Maule and R. D. Robinson, *Dual Loyalty* (Toronto: McGraw-Hill Book Co., 1971), p. 149.
23. Toronto *Globe and Mail,* June 21, 1972.
24. *Foreign Direct Investment,* p. 514.
25. Toronto *Globe and Mail,* June 17, 1972.
26. Toronto *Daily Star,* September 15, 1972.
27. House of Commons *Debates,* March 21, 1972, p. 1,000.
28. House of Commons *Debates,* November 22, 1971, p. 9,773.
29. House of Commons *Debates,* May 23, 1972, p. 2,464.
30. House of Commons *Debates,* December 9, 1971, p. 10,335.
31. *Eleventh Report of the Standing Committee,* p. 66.
32. Toronto *Globe and Mail,* February 4, 1972.
33. Speech to Canadian Manufacturers' Association Annual Meeting, Edmonton, June 5, 1972.
34. *Minutes,* Standing Committee on Finance, Trade and Economic Affairs, Fourth Session, Twenty-eighth Parliament, June 20, 1972, p. 15.
35. House of Commons *Debates,* January 4, 1973, p. 5.
36. House of Commons *Debates,* January 10, 1972, p. 154.

Appendix 1

A BRIEF CHRONOLOGY OF KEY EVENTS IN THE EVOLUTION
OF CANADIAN POLICY ON FOREIGN DIRECT INVESTMENT

Federal Government

1957 *Canadian and British Insurance Companies Act*
Majority of the board of directors must be Canadian. Directors granted the power to refuse to allow the transfer of shares
from a resident to a nonresident citizen.

1958 *Royal Commission on Canada's Economic Prospects
(Gordon Report)*
First officially posed the question of foreign ownership as an
issue requiring government policy decisions and intervention.
The report recommended action to increase the degree of
Canadian control of the foreign subsidiaries by a greater inclusion of Canadians in management and boards of directors,
an increase of Canadian equity in subsidiaries, and the publication of financial reports.

Broadcasting Act
Set a limit of 25 percent on foreign ownership of TV broadcasting undertakings (excluding cable television).

1960 *Canadian Participation Provisions (CPP)*
First introduced in 1960 as a part of the Canada Oil and Gas
Land Regulations and the Canada Mining Regulations, pur-
suant to the Territorial Lands Act and the Public Lands
Grants Act. Oil and gas and mining leases, under the CPP,
granted only to persons who are Canadian citizens over
twenty-one years of age and to Canadian corporations with

a) at least 50 percent of the issue shares beneficially owned
by Canadians citizens, *or*

b) shares listed on a recognized Canadian stock exchange,
and Canadians having an opportunity to participate in the
ownership of the corporation.

1962 *Corporations and Labour Unions Returns Act (CALURA)*
Empowered the government to collect financial and other information on the affairs of corporations and labor unions
carrying on activities in Canada.

1963 *Air Regulations Act*
To be a registered owner of a Canadian aircraft, at least two-
thirds of a corporation's directors must be Canadian citizens.

Walter Gordon's first budget of the new Liberal government
headed by Lester Pearson included the strongest measures
ever directed toward foreign ownership of Canadian business
corporations. A 30 percent tax was to be levied on the value
of shares of Canadian firms listed on stock exchanges sold to
nonresident corporations. To further encourage Canadian
ownership, the 15 percent withholding tax on dividends paid
to nonresidents was to be reduced to 10 percent for companies whose shares were at least one-quarter Canadian-
owned, and increased to 20 percent for firms with a lower
proportion of domestic ownership. Gordon also proposed a
faster rate of depreciation to companies with the requisite
25 percent Canadian ownership. A few days later, after strong
pressure from the financial community had been brought to
bear on him, Gordon announced the withdrawal of the takeover tax and the second portion of the withholding tax
change, but the other provisions were enacted.

1964 *Insurance and Loan and Trust Companies Acts (amendments)*
Limited the proportion of shares in these concerns owned by
nonresidents to no more than 25 percent; at least three-

fourths of the directors had to be Canadian citizens resident in Canada.

Radio Act
Radio and cable television placed on the same basis as TV, regulated in the 1958 Broadcasting Act.

1965 *Income Tax Act and Customs Act*
The Income Tax Act affected the establishment of new foreign-controlled newspapers and periodicals and the foreign takeover of existing newspapers and periodicals under Canadian control. In computing taxable income, no deduction could be made for the cost of advertising directed primarily at the Canadian market in an issue of a non-Canadian newspaper or periodical. Exemptions were made for *Time* and *Reader's Digest*.

The Customs Act change had the effect of prohibiting entry of non-Canadian periodicals containing advertisements directed at the Canadian market.

1966 *Guiding Principles of Good Corporate Citizenship for Foreign Subsidiaries (The Winters Guidelines,* see Appendix 2)
Sent to all foreign-owned companies by Robert Winters, Minister of Trade and Commerce.

Territorial Lands Act, Public Lands Grants Act, and Canada Mining Regulations
Leases of lands in the Northwest Territories and public lands to be granted only to persons of Canadian citizenship or corporations owned at least 50 percent by Canadian citizens.

Territorial Lands Act, Public Lands Grants Act, Canada Oil and Gas Land Regulations
Oil and gas leases to be granted only to persons of Canadian citizenship or corporations owned at least 50 percent by Canadian citizens.

1967 *Bank Act*
At least three-fourths of the directors of banks must be Canadian citizens; proportion of shares held by nonresidents limited to 25 percent; no one person to hold more than 10 percent of the shares; and no foreigners allowed to start up a new bank. Growth limits placed on banks presently having more than 25 percent foreign ownership, a provision specifically applying to the Mercantile Bank, 100 percent of which

was then owned by the First National City Bank of New York. In 1971, Mercantile and the Canadian government agreed to a plan for sale of new stock to Canadians to result in 75 percent Canadian ownership by 1980.

1968 *Broadcasting Act (amendment)*
The Canadian broadcasting system must be owned and controlled by Canadians in order to "safeguard, enrich and strengthen the cultural, political, social and economic fabric of Canada." Licenses to be issued or renewals granted only to Canadian citizens and eligible Canadian corporations.

Report on Foreign Ownership and the Structure of Canadian Industry (Watkins Report)
The report of a task force of professors appointed by a cabinet committee headed by Walter Gordon. Recommendations included:

1) establishing a special agency to coordinate policies concerning the multinational enterprise;
2) establishing a government export trade agency to ensure that export orders were filled when they conformed with Canadian law and Canadian foreign policy;
3) creating a Canada Development Corporation to act as a large holding company with entrepreneurial and management functions to assume a leadership role in Canada's business community.

1970 *Report of Commons Standing Committee on External Affairs and National Defence (Wahn Report)*
Recommendations on foreign ownership, including requirement that major subsidiaries sell 51 percent of stock to Canadians.

Canada Corporations Act
Foreign companies required to publish annual reports.

Loan Companies Act
1. At least 75 percent of the directors must be Canadian citizens.
2. Shares held by nonresidents restricted to 25 percent.
3. Voting rights of nonresidents by nominees or by proxy prohibited.

1971 *Investment Companies Act*
Foreign ownership of federally incorporated sales finance firms limited to 25 percent.

1972 *Foreign Direct Investment in Canada (Gray Report)*
Three broad strategies for dealing with foreign investments
were examined, with the first recommended as the primary
policy approach.

1. Screening by a government agency to block investment
    that does not make a net contribution to the Canadian
    economy.
2. Delineation of further "key sectors" in which foreign own-
    ership would be regulated.
3. Introduction of across-the-board ownership rules (e.g.,
    51 percent Canadian ownership of all firms) and other
    structural changes relating to the use of Canadian man-
    agers and directors.

Foreign Takeovers Review Bill (proposed but not enacted)
All acquisitions by foreign investors of Canadian firms with
assets of more than $250,000 or gross revenues of more than
$3 million would be subject to review by the cabinet.

1973 *Speech from the Throne*
Statement of government legislative plan opening the new
Parliament. Included proposals to screen takeovers immediately, to improve access to foreign technology for Canadian
business, to increase Canadian participation in resource projects, to require a majority of Canadians on boards of directors, and, in consultation with the provinces, to develop measures to deal with new foreign investment.

Foreign Investment Review Bill
Introduced in the House of Commons, January 24. Would
establish a Foreign Investment Review Agency and make all
new foreign direct investments subject to review except those
by companies already established in Canada within their existing line of business. Immediately upon enactment, review
would commence for takeovers by foreign investors of Canadian firms above the size limits as in the 1972 proposed bill.
At a date to be proclaimed by the government, review would
be extended to establishment of new businesses by foreign
investors not already doing business in Canada and opening
of new businesses by existing foreign-controlled firms in Canada in unrelated lines of activity. Upon this proclamation the
size thresholds for takeover review would be eliminated. Approval of investments would be based upon demonstration
that they would be beneficial to Canada by several stated

criteria. The agency would make recommendations to the Minister of Industry, Trade and Commerce, who would advise the cabinet; the latter would make the final review decisions.

Ontario Government

1970 Nonresident equity participation restricted in loan and trust companies.

1971 1. Periodical and Paperback Distributors Act restricted foreign equity participation.
2. Government extended financial assistance to the publishing firm McClelland & Stewart to lessen possibility of acquisition by foreign interests.
3. Nonresident equity participation restricted in securities industry.
4. Ontario Development Corporation regulations altered to favor Canadian-owned enterprises.
5. Government remitted sales tax to facilitate repatriation of Adams Iron Ore Mine.

1972 1. *Report of the Select Committee on Economic and Cultural Nationalism, Ontario Legislative Assembly* Recommendations included:
   a) support the development of an industrial strategy to encourage internationally competitive industries;
   b) a minimum of 20 percent of the directors of all foreign companies shall be Canadian citizens;
   c) measures should be taken to control the sale of Canadian firms where no public benefit would result from foreign ownership.
2. Forgivable loans to foreign-owned firms were suspended pending a review of the program.
3. Amendments to the Business Corporations Act proposed to require that a majority of the boards of directors of Ontario companies be resident Canadians by October 1, 1973, that there be a Canadian at each meeting, and that a majority of board meetings be held in Canada.
4. An investment capital information service was established to match entrepreneurship with Canadian capital sources.

Appendix 2

1. Pursuit of sound growth and full realization of the company's productive potential, thereby sharing the national objective of full and effective use of the nation's resources.

2. Realization of maximum competitiveness through the most effective use of the company's own resources, recognizing the desirability of progressively achieving appropriate specialization of productive operations within the internationally affiliated group of companies.

3. Maximum development of market opportunities in other countries as well as in Canada.

4. Where applicable, to extend processing of natural-resource products to the extent practicable on an economic basis.

5. Pursuit of a pricing policy designed to assure a fair and reasonable return to the company and to Canada for all goods and services sold abroad, including sales to the parent company and other foreign affiliates.

6. In matters of procurement, to search out and develop economic sources of supply in Canada.

7. To develop as an integral part of the Canadian operation, wherever practicable, the technological, research and design capability necessary to enable the company to pursue appropriate product development programs so as to take full advantage of market opportunities domestically and abroad.

8. Retention of a sufficient share of earnings to give appropriate financial support to the growth requirements of the Canadian operation, having in mind a fair return to shareholders on capital invested.

9. To work toward a Canadian outlook within management, through purposeful training programs, promotion of qualified Canadian personnel, and inclusion of a major proportion of Canadian citizens on its board of directors.

10. To have the objective of a financial structure which provides opportunity for equity participation in the Canadian enterprise by the Canadian public.

11. Periodically to publish information on the financial position and operations of the company.

12. To give appropriate attention and support to recognized national objectives and established government programs designed to further Canada's economic development and to encourage and support Canadian institutions directed toward the intellectual, social, and cultural advancement of the community.

Appendix 3

THE EVOLUTION OF POSITIONS ON FOREIGN
INVESTMENT POLICY IN THE MAIN POLITICAL
PARTIES FROM 1966 TO 1972

A‌s general public opinion in Canada on foreign investment policy
has shifted, so have positions within the political parties. Therefore,
recognizing the key role of political leaders in government decisions,
I directed substantial research effort to trying to identify these positions and determine their trend. This effort proved exceptionally
frustrating. In part the problem lay in the heterogeneous character of
the two major parties described in Chapter 2, which makes it hard
to determine anything that can be characterized as *the* party position
at any one time. And in part it is difficult to find statements that are
useful for this purpose, that have sufficient authority and compre-
hensiveness. There are just a few official party policy statements.
Otherwise one must work from a hodgepodge of speeches by leaders,
policy recommendations by party subgroups, and other material
which is less than authoritative and comprehensive. One reaction to
this situation would be to confine one's report to a very limited number of issues on which official positions were clear. The discussion in
Chapter 2 essentially embodies that approach. But having invested
substantial effort in the broader survey of the history of views in the
parties, I think it useful to report the results, and this appendix has
that intent.

The basic concept of the material which follows is that, even though any one speech or other statement may lack clear authority or completeness in dealing with foreign investment policy, the aggregate character of many such expressions of views gives one a picture of the trend of thinking within a party. A simplified composite picture for the Liberals, Conservatives, and New Democratic Party is presented in Charts 3–5. Each notes in abbreviated form the positions taken on certain recurring aspects of foreign investment policy in either individual statements or collections of speeches over limited periods, which in composite seemed to convey the main focus of interest of party leaders. In addition, a brief narrative history is provided to give some sense of the evolution of views which the bare facts in the charts do not convey. The Social Credit Party was not included because, as a practical matter, it has not been a major power factor in national decision making. Nor has it appeared particularly interested in foreign investment policy.

Liberal Party

The starting point for this history of the recent evolution of Liberal Party views is the publication, in March 1966, of "Some Guiding Principles of Good Corporate Behavior" by Robert Winters, then Minister of Trade and Commerce. The full text of the principles appears on pages 175–76, and the key points are noted in Chart 3. Fundamentally this action was indicative of the prevailing Liberal viewpoint that, except in key sectors, the activities of foreign-owned firms should be subject only to persuasive influence.

This philosophy was explicit in resolutions adopted at the October 1966 party convention. The overall policy decision was: "The government should take steps to encourage greater ownership of the economy, without discouraging foreign investment." Other than affirming the Winters Guidelines, the convention emphasized the steps listed in Chart 1 which might build up Canadian-owned firms. One resolution also specified that "our main objective should be to create the conditions conducive to a continuing rising standard of living," by implication indicating that assertion of greater control of national affairs at the expense of economically productive foreign investment was not desirable. The sole policy on energy stated that exports should be increased to improve the balance of payments.

A speech by Robert Winters in January 1967 followed this same general tack, advocating positive steps to foster Canadian firms, not "negative or punitive legislation affecting foreign interests." He also spoke of the Canadian desire to mutually improve access for goods between Canada and the United States. External Affairs Minister Paul Martin, in a speech in the same month, had similar views but with a slightly new twist: "We must provide the legal and policy framework in which the foreign investors can make the maximum possible contribution to our national welfare."

During the 1968 election campaign, foreign investment was rarely mentioned, but some minor comments are informative. In May, Trudeau made a speech saying there should be no controls on foreign investment but that incentives should be given to steering it in directions that contribute most to Canada's economic growth. In a June television debate among Trudeau, Stanfield, and Douglas, the first stated that he could support "all of the aims of the Watkins report." He specifically mentioned only the requirement of greater public financial reporting. He gave greater emphasis to building up Canadian enterprises, especially in industries where Canada could achieve greatest benefits.

The year 1969 was more notable for concrete events demonstrating the thrust of Liberal policy than for new viewpoints. An Investment Companies Act was proposed which would prevent nonresidents from holding more than 25 percent of financing companies as a result of future transactions, i.e., existing ownership patterns would not be affected. Amendments were proposed to the Canada Corporations Act requiring public financial statements. And in response to comments about the takeover of a major Canadian firm, Industry Minister Pepin protested that present law precluded action but that there was concern insofar as it was hoped that the proposed Canada Development Corporation would be able to play a role to relieve such situations.

During 1969 there was increasing attention to issues now subsumed under "industrial strategy," and this trend continued into 1970. Pepin, for example, spoke at length in January 1970 about such things as support for Canadian R&D and pressures by the Canadian government for more exports and continental rationalization, "the need for 'parents' to integrate their Canadian plants in their world and North American complexes." In a February 21 interview reported in *Le Monde,* Trudeau prescribed as a strategy for escaping American domination that Canada invest more in sectors where it could play a major role rather than try to cover the whole field, the "product niche" concept discussed in Chapter 4.

The year 1970 was also interesting in the expression of certain viewpoints which indicated strong internal pressures within the party. In June, a paper on industrial policy objectives by MP Alistair Gillespie (subsequently to become a cabinet minister) was distributed among a number of Liberals. He proposed that in future resource development, Canadians have 50 percent ownership and that foreign takeovers be subject to Canadian government approval. The Wahn Report appeared, supported by the Liberal majority on a Commons committee endorsing requirement of majority Canadian ownership of major firms. Energy Minister J. J. Greene made a strongly nationalistic speech in Denver in May, asserting that in the future Canadians would require greater participation in resource development. This speech was particularly notable as in it Greene reported his own change of attitude: "I for one have come but lately to the conviction that a growing degree of Canadian ownership . . . was essential to the maintenance of Canada as a free, viable and independent nation." From the greater frequency of expressions of opinion on this subject and their tone, one could sense that this was a period of substantial reorientation of thinking within the party toward a stronger effort to assert Canadian interest and identity in the foreign investment situation.

The year also saw Herb Gray start work on his report, indicating an official Liberal intent to come to grips with the policy issues. Finally, in November there was a party convention at which 1,649 delegates voted on a number of resolutions concerning foreign investments. The general thrust of the votes was clearly for a stronger line than the party leadership was prepared to adopt, including screening all investments and creating special classes of voting shares to permit majority Canadian control of foreign-owned firms.

Other than the leaked version of the Gray Report, 1971 did not, for the most part, produce any notable statements indicating further development of Liberal thinking on foreign investments. The only other conspicuous pronouncement was Trudeau's observation in an October interview that he felt 60 percent control of Canadian industry by foreigners should be considered the maximum tolerable level. The few other statements which did appear on the subject were more notable as indications of recognition of the difficulties of implementing the inclinations toward stronger policies evident in the previous year. Prime Minister Trudeau was quite candid on this count in a November press conference. He observed that at a recent meeting with provincial premiers, substantial objections to the idea of screening investments had been voiced. More important was the shock effect of the U.S. economic moves on August 15 in relation to

Canada's economic condition. Speaking about basic foreign investment policy, Trudeau observed: "I dare say if we had made a decision
six months ago, it might have been marginally different than a decision we might make in six weeks . . . I do know that since the Nixon
measures and . . . since the latest unemployment figures . . . that
there's much greater circumspection in Canada on the degree of
toughness with which we want to treat foreign capital here. As I've
often said in speeches of various kinds, Canadians had now reached
a trade-off point where they were perhaps wealthy enough to begin
to be able to pick and choose the degree of foreign economic domination. And my statement was that the more affluent we were the
freer we were to make the choice. And I think it would be unrealistic to say the choice would be exactly the same . . . at a time of
high employment and at a time of low employment."

Speeches by Pepin, Sharp, and the new Energy Minister, Donald
Macdonald, in early 1972 indicated continued effort within the Liberal leadership to compromise nationalistic desires with other practical conditions. In one way or another, they indicated a desire to
maintain Canada's favorable foreign-investment-climate image as a
basis for continued inflow of capital. On the other hand, they argued
the logics of some controls, e.g., Sharp to the American Management Association: "I find no contradiction in supporting some limitations on the operations of foreign-controlled corporations in Canada."
The thrust toward a mild screening process was evident, for example,
in Macdonald's comments: "I favour a pragmatic look at the advantages and disadvantages of any particular investment action proposed
for our economy with foreign investment having the onus of demonstrating its contributions to our Canadian well-being and to the
aspirations of Canadians."

In May the Gray Report and the proposed Foreign Takeovers
Review bill gave a concrete picture of the status of Liberal views.
Their orientation was discussed in Chapter 5. In the historical perspective taken here, the Gray Report would seem to represent a fair
consensus of party desires to achieve greater control of the economy,
but via the route of direct control over the activities of foreign firms
in order to maximize benefits to Canada rather than through special
efforts to inject Canadian equity participation in them. The takeovers
bill carried the practical compromising process further by limiting
the intervention to an area that would create minimum problems
both with the provinces and industrial growth in general.

The Liberal Party did not press foreign investment policy in the
1972 campaign, evidently satisfied to rest on its record with no ver-
bal development of its position.

Progressive Conservative Party

Lacking any significant statements on foreign investment policy in 1966, we start the Conservative section of this history with the 1967 party convention. The chairman's report had a brief but pithy treatment of foreign investment. It sought economic improvement by stimulation of "investment, whether foreign or domestic." Emphasis was given to incentives to encourage Canadians to invest at home. The Canada Development Corporation was rejected "in favour of the efficiency of the private market-place" and more use of the Industrial Development Bank.

The policy handbook and one statement by party leader Robert Stanfield were the only good sources of Conservative thinking available for the 1968 election period. They continued the philosophy of encouraging all types of investment through helping Canadian-owned industry to foster national investment. The exception to the general philosophy was the clear support for Canadian control of key sectors.

A notable feature of 1969 was a speech in May by a prominent Conservative, MP J. W. Montieth, proposing that takeovers must meet a set of tests to prove they were beneficial to Canada, essentially the same concept as the 1972 takeovers bill (though a screening system was not explicitly advocated). A statement by Stanfield in July reasserted the basically open investment policy, subject to the key sector exception.

In October 1969, a party policy convention committee failed to reach agreement on a proposed foreign investment report. While not official party policy, its contents give an indication of the direction of some Conservative thinking, though there were members who strongly opposed it. The general concept of openness to foreign capital was endorsed, but with notable constraints: new resource investments were to require 50 percent Canadian equity; "legally enforceable standards of corporate behaviour should be established"; and full financial disclosure was supported. An oddity in this relatively nationalistic report was the support of "a true continental oil and gas policy based on economic mutual interest." The authors doubtless did not perceive the hazardous "continentalist" flavor of the statement and were emphasizing the last phrase, benefits to Canada being the assumed outcome. A speech by Stanfield in November noted the failure of the conference to agree on a statement and essentially affirmed the policy of nondiscrimination against foreign firms and control of key sectors.

Two speeches by Stanfield in 1970 dealt broadly with the foreign investment situation and added no specific positions to those
previously stated. One senses in the space devoted to the subject and
in the tenor of the comments some growing belief in the importance
of the issues and a desire to project an image that the Conservatives
were deeply concerned, even if their specific proposals were still
quite limited. Stanfield argued also that a clear policy was needed,
since uncertainty would discourage investment.

An early 1971 Stanfield speech followed much the same line but
added a significant paragraph noting "that ownership and control
are not necessarily the same thing." The basic goal he prescribed
was "to make sure that the essential levers of control are in the
hands of Canadians." When the Canada Development Corporation
bill was presented to Commons, the Conservatives opposed it for
the reasons outlined in Chapter 2.

In May, a series of papers proposing policy positions were circulated among the party leaders for discussion. One on "Canadian
Identity" dealt with a wide range of aspects of foreign investment
policy along quite strong nationalistic lines. Policies that required
Canadian members of boards of directors and the screening of takeovers were advanced for the first time in a party document.

In November the Conservatives placed a non-confidence motion
before the House of Commons that included criticism of the government "for failing to develop a new economic policy which would
strengthen our economic independence and fully employ our growing and highly-skilled human resources." MP Gordon Fairweather,
a leading Conservative, spoke to the foreign investment implications
of this motion, so his comments give some indication of party views
even though he was clearly speaking as an individual who, by his
membership in the Committee for an Independent Canada, could be
placed in the more nationalistic wing of his party. He labeled extraterritorial application of foreign laws as "the major issue." His prescription for a new national economic policy consisted of more
processing of natural resources, greater R&D, incentives to switch
savings to equity investment, an explicit policy on resource development, exploitation of bargaining power gained from resources, and
coordination with the provinces. He also labeled as problems the
extent of takeovers and the large portion of federal grants going to
foreign-owned firms, but he suggested no policies on these matters.

At the party's annual general meeting in December the delegates
voted on a series of proposals. Those dealing with foreign investment
were endorsed by a very substantial majority. Their thrust was generally along the lines of the discussion paper circulated earlier in the

year, though the latter sounded somewhat tougher in character, perhaps because it spelled out implications of policies in greater detail. There was also no proposal offered to the meeting on the general screening of takeovers, suggesting that the party leadership did not wish it to be adopted.

Three speeches by Stanfield at the start of 1972 stuck to a consistent line. He strongly opposed a general screening system which would restrict the inflow of foreign capital. He also emphasized the divisive effects of any system which did not give a strong voice to the provinces. He did acknowledge the value of some degree of regulation of foreign investment, especially in the key sectors, but placed the emphasis for action on building up Canadian firms.

When the Foreign Takeovers Review bill was presented, Stanfield accepted the screening concept in principle, provided there were adequate guidelines and provincial consultation. He stressed, however, that priority should go to building up Canadian firms, disclosure by foreign-owned firms, and requiring Canadian participation on boards of directors. The formal Conservative position set forth by MP Gordon Fairweather is discussed in Chapter 2. Essentially it appeared that the Conservatives were accepting the idea of screening takeovers, but they were minimizing the importance of the step and pointing out its weaknesses, especially in provincial relations. The thrust was toward emphasizing the other areas of possible action brought out in Stanfield's speeches.

Finally, there were the policy papers released by the Conservatives at the end of the 1972 campaign. Most of the specific steps proposed were in line with the positions taken by Stanfield previously, i.e., Canadianization of boards, provincial consultation, etc. The takeover review principle was accepted implicitly by criticizing the Liberal plan only for its lack of provincial consultation. The only new items had minor implications—support of more debt vs. equity in new foreign capital input and encouragement to "buy Canadian" programs.

New Democratic Party

While the two previous histories start in the mid-1960s, it is interesting in the case of the New Democratic Party to go a bit further back. At the 1961 party convention, a resolution was adopted that the NDP "seeks to break monopoly control over Canadian industry and resources," with particular attention to the foreign-owned firms. For this purpose the party would require a minimum percentage of Canadian ownership and representation on boards of directors, and the government should "negotiate over a period of years the selective repatriation of Canada's resources and industries." The convention also proposed a Canadian Development Fund to mobilize public and pension fund capital for industrial development and research.

The 1967 convention expressed the same degree of concern about foreign-owned investment, but its proposals took a quite different direction. There was no mention of requirements for Canadian ownership or board membership. The main emphasis was on increased government participation in industry and, specifically, the creation of a Capital Resources Fund with essentially the same character as the fund proposed in 1961. The emphasis had changed from repatriation and direct control of foreign firms to direct public efforts to force-feed the Canadian-owned sector.

This change of direction was affirmed in a 1968 campaign document which declared: "It is already too late to think in terms of 'buying back' those Canadian industries already owned by foreigners. What can be done, however, is to adopt laws and policies compelling such industries to operate in a manner conducive to the best interests of Canada, rather than of foreign firms or governments, while at the same time stimulating more investment in and ownership of future economic development." The Watkins Report was specifically endorsed, and the main vehicle proposed for the future again was the Capital Resources Fund, whose capital would be reinforced by exchange controls to check the outflow of Canadian savings to the United States.

Speeches by David Lewis and T. C. Douglas in 1969 indicated that the NDP leadership was adhering to this general tack but with some detailed shifts. Support for the Canada Development Corporation was expressed, and the Capital Resources Fund was no longer mentioned. The concept of the CDC was similar to that anticipated for the fund. Some effort to attain Canadian equity participation in foreign-owned firms reappeared, ending with a new proposal for an agency to serve as a watchdog over foreign firms. Lewis' speech to Commons in May was conspicuous in the total national evolution of thinking because he forced attention on key issues raised in the Watkins Report, which had been released two months earlier but which the Liberals had tended to play down.

At the NDP convention in October, the so-called Waffle Manifesto was presented. Since the Wafflers never achieved acceptance by the full NDP, it does not represent the party position. In the present discussion, therefore, it is significant chiefly as a gauge of the limits beyond which the NDP was not prepared to go. The manifesto was devoted almost entirely to stating the bad effects of domination by foreign-owned companies. The action program was confined to two brief paragraphs at the end. Their essence was that the objective should be a socialist society, including "nationalization of the commanding heights of the economy, such as key resource industries, finance and credit, and industries strategic to planning our economy." This basic goal was rejected by the NDP in a speech by David Lewis late that month, in which he observed that "many years ago, our party rejected the idea that public ownership is a panacea for all ills."

The resolutions adopted by the convention essentially followed the tack the leaders had been setting forth, except that they did for the first time explicitly support screening of takeovers and advanced the concept of "public and co-operative ownership to promote ownership by Canadians of a larger sector of the economy." The implementation of the concept was elaborated only in broad terms, but the basic philosophy was clearly that the control of foreign firms was to be achieved by some degree of government ownership along with strong economic direction, as distinguished from the full nationalization proposed by the Wafflers. The CDC would fit into this scheme as a government-directed economic initiative center and financial capital source.

Two speeches by Douglas in early 1970 repeated for the most part the 1969 positions. The one new feature was advocacy of an amendment to the corporations act limiting foreign ownership to 25 percent. While this would apply only to future firms and takeovers, it was a much stronger step than his mild encouragement in 1969 that foreign firms offer shares to Canadians. This position was explicitly repeated in the official NDP commentary on the Wahn Report, which the party endorsed but felt to be too mild. The other new point in the commentary was that federal grants should be made to foreign firms only in exceptional cases.

In January 1971, speeches by Douglas and Lewis showed that the NDP views were moving to a yet stronger approach to foreign investment. The chief addition was the proposal of "strict rules regulating the expansion of foreign-owned corporations."

When the Canada Development Corporation bill reached Commons in February, NDP spokesman Max Saltsman cut it to pieces, castigating it as "a gesture for propaganda purposes." As an independent, essentially private management entity, it in no way served the intent for which the NDP had been striving.

The NDP convention in April gave primary attention to the natural resource sector of foreign investment. Apart from the vigor of its presentation, it adds nothing to our picture of the party. The main points of greater public control and ownership and avoidance of continental energy deals had been expressed for some time.

In December, Lewis outlined a program for independence for Canada, largely repeating previous points but adding one new one, a requirement of full disclosure of facts before a plant shut down so the government could have the option of taking it over. He also called for a major restructuring of the CDC to fit the concept of the NDP.

When the takeovers bill was presented, Lewis criticized it as entirely inadequate and went on to present the latest NDP program. The party thinking had reached a yet stronger level in advocating the use of $5 billion of foreign exchange reserves to repatriate ownership of some foreign-owned firms and assorted measures to indirectly discourage new foreign capital inflow.

Chart 3
Positions on Foreign Investment and Related Industrial Strategy Policies: LIBERAL PARTY

(**Y** — Policy supported, **N** — Policy opposed, **E** — Action should be encouraged, **R** — Action should be required)

	1966		1967	1968	1969	1970					1971	1972		
	1	2	3	4	5	6	7	8	9	10	11	12	13	14
Foreign Investment														
a. "Buy back" foreign subsidiaries									N		N			
b. Canadian equity in subsidiaries	E	E							E	E			E	
c. Check flow of new foreign investment		N					N			N	N			
d. Limit takeovers					E			E	E				Y	Y
e. Screen investments: General										Y		E	Y	
Takeovers								Y		Y			Y	Y
f. More debt vs. equity		Y								Y				
g. Limit grants to subsidiaries														
h. Expand key sectors						Y				Y		Y	Y	
i. More control over subsidiaries			E							Y		E		
j. Improve behavior of subsidiaries	E	E	E			E	E	E					Y	E
k. Agency to monitor behavior										Y				
l. Canadian majority on boards of directors	E	E											E	E
m. Require more financial disclosure	E	E		R	R					R				
n. More exports by subsidiaries	E	E			E		E						Y	E
o. More R&D by subsidiaries	E	E										E	E	E
p. Give information on plant shutdowns														
q. Obey Canadian laws			R								Y			
r. Avoid extraterritorial law application			E			E	E			Y		Y	Y	
s. Develop multinational control of MNCs					E		E			Y		Y	Y	
Industrial Strategy														
a. Encourage development of Canadian firms			E	E			E						Y	
b. Expand public sector														
c. Increase Canadian investment in industry: General		Y							Y		Y			
By financial institutions		E												
d. Divert outflow of capital for domestic use		E												
e. Greater use of Industrial Development Bank		Y												
f. Create Canada Development Corporation		Y		Y	Y		Y	Y		Y	Y			
g. Create Capital Resource Fund														
h. Pick special fields for industrial development				Y		Y						Y		
i. Rationalization: Within Canada					Y					Y				
Continental	E	Y			Y	Y				Y				
j. Increased R&D		Y				Y	Y		Y		Y ·	Y	Y	
k. Foster entrepreneurship and management								Y		Y	Y	Y		Y
l. Establish "buy Canadian" rules	E	E												
m. Develop Canadian MNCs						Y	Y	Y	Y					
n. Resources: More processing in Canada	E	E												
Avoid continental energy policy										Y				

Notes to Chart 3

Numbers identify the numbered statements listed across the top of the chart.

1. Robert Winters, Minister of Trade and Commerce, "Some Guiding Principles of Good Corporate Conduct," March 31, 1966.

2. Resolutions adopted at the national Liberal Party meeting, Ottawa, October 10–12, 1966.

3. Robert Winters, speech at joint meeting of Canadian-American Association and World Affairs Council, San Francisco, California, January 24, 1967; Paul Martin, Secretary of State for External Affairs, speech at Vancouver Board of Trade, January 18, 1967; and Lester Pearson, Prime Minister, television speech, February 1, 1967.

4. Pierre Trudeau, Prime Minister, speech at Kitchener-Waterloo, May 1968, and television appearance, June 9, 1968.

5. E. J. Benson, Minister of Finance, House of Commons *Debates,* May 29, 1968, p. 9,222; Jean-Luc Pepin, Minister of Industry, Trade and Commerce, speech to the British Society of Chemical Industry, Ottawa, September 18, 1969; and Ron Basford, Minister of Consumer and Corporate Affairs, House of Commons *Debates,* November 10, 1969.

6. E. J. Benson, press release, January 21, 1970; Jean-Luc Pepin, speech to Toronto Board of Trade, January 26, 1970; and Pierre Trudeau, interview, *Le Monde,* February 21, 1970.

7. Herb Gray, Minister of National Revenue, speech to Osgoode Law Society, April 8, 1970.

8. Alastair Gillespie, discussion paper circulated by Liberal Party, June 1970.

9. P. Mahoney, Parliamentary Secretary to Minister of Finance, speech to Charlottestown Board of Trade, Prince Edward Island, November 19, 1970.

10. Resolutions adopted at national Liberal Party convention, Ottawa, November 20–22, 1970.

11. E. J. Benson, House of Commons *Debates,* February 22, 1971, p. 3,637; and P. Mahoney, speech to Tax Executives Institute, February 25, 1971; Jean-Luc Pepin, speech in Houston, Texas, September 29, 1971; Pierre Trudeau, interview, Ottawa *Citizen,* October 29, 1971; and Pierre Trudeau, press conference, November 17, 1971.

12. Mitchell Sharp, Minister of State for External Affairs, speech to American Management Association, February 3, 1972; Speech from the Throne, House of Commons *Debates,* February 17, 1972; Donald Macdonald, Minister of Energy, Mines and Resources, House of Commons *Debates,* February 24, 1972, p. 222; and Jean-Luc Pepin, speech at Mid-America World Trade Conference, Chicago, March 1, 1972.

13. *Foreign Direct Investment in Canada,* Government of Canada, 1972.

14. Bill C-201, Fourth Session, Twenty-Eighth Parliament.

Chart 4

Positions on Foreign Investment and Related Industrial Strategy Policies: PROGRESSIVE CONSERVATIVE PARTY

(**Y** — Policy supported, **N** — Policy opposed, **E** — Action should be encouraged, **R** — Action should be required)

	1967	1968	1969			1970	1971				1972				
	1	2	3	4	5	6	7	8	9	10	11	12	13	14	15
Foreign Investment															
a. "Buy back" foreign subsidiaries	N						N								
b. Canadian equity in subsidiaries															
c. Check flow of new foreign investment	N	N		N						N	N				
d. Limit takeovers															
e. Screen investments: General											N				
Takeovers			Y				Y				Y	Y			Y
f. More debt vs. equity				Y											Y
g. Limit grants to subsidiaries															
h. Expand key sectors		Y	Y		Y		Y			Y	Y	Y	Y	Y	Y
i. More control over subsidiaries							Y				Y				
j. Improve behavior of subsidiaries				Y			Y		Y				Y		
k. Agency to monitor behavior															
l. Canadian majority on boards of directors							Y			Y		Y	Y	Y	Y
m. Require more financial disclosure				Y		Y	Y			Y		Y	Y	Y	Y
n. More exports by subsidiaries							Y								
o. More R&D by subsidiaries							Y	Y							
p. Give information on plant shutdowns															
q. Obey Canadian laws															
r. Avoid extraterritorial law application		Y		Y		Y	Y	Y	Y					Y	Y
s. Develop multinational control of MNCs					Y	Y	Y	Y	Y				Y		Y
Industrial Strategy															
a. Encourage development of Canadian firms											Y	Y			Y
b. Expand public sector															
c. Increase Canadian investment in industry: General	Y	Y									Y	Y		Y	Y
By financial institutions	Y			Y			Y	Y	Y						
d. Divert outflow of capital for domestic use															
e. Greater use of Industrial Development Bank	Y			Y											
f. Create Canada Development Corporation	N					N									
g. Create Capital Resource Fund															
h. Pick special fields for industrial development							Y								Y
i. Rationalization: Within Canada															Y
Continental							Y								
j. Increased R&D							Y	Y							Y
k. Foster entrepreneurship and management				Y			Y		Y		Y				Y
l. Establish "buy Canadian" rules															E
m. Develop Canadian MNCs															
n. Resources: More processing in Canada						Y	Y								
Avoid continental energy policy				N	Y										

Notes to Chart 4

Numbers identify the numbered statements listed across the top of the chart.

1. Chairman's Report of Policy Committee, Progressive Conservative Party convention, September 5–7, 1967.
2. Policy Handbook, Progressive Conservative Party, 1968; and Robert Stanfield, television appearance, June 9, 1968.
3. J. W. Monteith, House of Commons *Debates,* May 29, 1969, p. 9,225; and Robert Stanfield, House of Commons *Debates,* July 2, 1972, p. 10,728.
4. Policy proposal, policy convention, Progressive Conservative Party, Niagara Falls, October 9–13, 1969.
5. Robert Stanfield, speech to Maple Leaf Dinner, New York, November 6, 1969.
6. Robert Stanfield, speeches to Toronto Senior Board of Trade, April 6, 1970, and in Renfrew, Ontario, October 3, 1970.
7. Robert Stanfield, speech to Edmonton East Progressive Conservative Association, March 30, 1971.
8. Press releases, Progressive Conservative Policy Co-ordinating Committee, May–July 1971, and Progressive Conservative Statement on Report of Standing Committee on External Affairs and National Defense, House of Commons, June 29, 1971.
9. Gordon Fairweather, House of Commons *Debates,* November 3, 1971, p. 9,312.
10. Resolutions, Progressive Conservative Party general meeting, December 5–7, 1971.
11. Robert Stanfield, speeches to Vancouver Board of Trade, January 24, 1972; in Halifax, February 5, 1972; and Hamilton, Ontario, February 16, 1972.
12. Robert Stanfield, House of Commons *Debates,* May 2, 1972, p. 1,829; and speech to Young Progressive Conservatives, Lake Couchichung, Ontario, May 13, 1972.
13. Gordon Fairweather, House of Commons *Debates,* May 29, 1972, p. 2,635.
14. Marcel Lambert, House of Commons *Debates,* May 29, 1972, p. 2,656; and David MacDonald, House of Commons *Debates,* May 30, p. 2,676.
15. Policy Papers, Progressive Conservative Party, October 1972.

Chart 5
Positions on Foreign Investment and Related Industrial Strategy Policies: NEW DEMOCRATIC PARTY
(**Y** — Policy supported, **N** — Policy opposed, **E** — Action should be encouraged; **R** — Action should be required)

	1967	1968	1969		1970			1971		1972
	1	2	3	4	5	6	7	8	9	10
Foreign Investment										
a. "Buy back" foreign subsidiaries					N		N			Y
b. Canadian equity in subsidiaries			Y		Y					
c. Check flow of new foreign investment										Y
d. Limit takeovers					Y		Y			
e. Screen investments: General							Y		Y	Y
Takeovers				Y						
f. More debt vs. equity										
g. Limit grants to subsidiaries						Y	Y			Y
h. Expand key sectors				Y	Y					
i. More control over subsidiaries										
j. Improve behavior of subsidiaries										
k. Agency to monitor behavior			Y		Y					
l. Canadian majority on boards of directors										
m. Require more financial disclosure	Y		Y	Y	Y					
n. More exports by subsidiaries										
o. More R&D by subsidiaries										
p. Give information on plant shutdowns									Y	Y
q. Obey Canadian laws										
r. Avoid extraterritorial law application		Y	Y	Y	Y		Y		Y	Y
s. Develop multinational control of MNCs										
Industrial Strategy										
a. Encourage development of Canadian firms					Y					
b. Expand public sector	Y			Y		Y	Y	Y	Y.	Y
c. Increase Canadian investment in industry: General	Y			Y			Y			
By financial institutions										
d. Divert outflow of capital for domestic use		Y								
e. Greater use of Industrial Development Bank										
f. Create Canada Development Corporation			Y	Y	Y	Y	Y			
g. Create Capital Resource Fund	Y	Y								
h. Pick special fields for industrial development										
i. Rationalization: Within Canada	Y	Y		Y					Y	Y
Continental										
j. Increased R&D	Y	Y		Y					Y	Y
k. Foster entrepreneurship and management										
l. Establish "buy Canadian" rules										
m. Develop Canadian MNCs										
n. Resources: More processing in Canada		Y						Y		Y
Avoid continental energy policy					Y		Y	Y		

Notes to Chart 5

Numbers identify the numbered statements listed across the top of the chart.

1. Resolutions, New Democratic Party convention, Toronto, 1967.
2. "Notes for Speakers," New Democratic Party, 1968.
3. David Lewis, House of Commons *Debates,* May 29, 1969, p. 9,216; and T. C. Douglas, speech to Canadian Club, Victoria, British Columbia, September 21, 1969.
4. Resolutions, New Democratic Party convention, Winnipeg, October 1969.
5. T. C. Douglas, news conference, January 13, 1970; CBC television interview, March 21, 1970; and speech at Beth Tzedic Synagogue, April 13, 1970.
6. NDP commentary on Report of Standing Committee on External Affairs and National Defense, House of Commons, July 31, 1970.
7. T. C. Douglas, press statement, January 12, 1971; David Lewis, speech, Winnipeg, January 28, 1971; and Max Saltsman, House of Commons *Debates,* February 22, 1971, p. 3,645.
8. Resolutions, New Democratic Party convention, April 12–24, 1971.
9. David Lewis, House of Commons *Debates,* December 9, 1971, p. 10,313.
10. David Lewis, House of Commons *Debates,* May 29, 1972, p. 2,639.

Explanations of Policies on Charts 3–5

Foreign Investment

a. "Buy back" foreign subsidiaries: A major government program to achieve substantial repatriation of foreign-owned firms.

b. Canadian equity in subsidiaries: Efforts to increase the portion of shares of foreign-owned firms held by Canadians

c. Check flow of new foreign investment: Actions which would reduce the inflow of new capital.

d. Limit takeovers: Actions to reduce the number of acquisitions of Canadian firms by foreign-owned companies.

e. Screen investments: A review system to check either all new investments, expansions, and other significant investments by foreign firms or just takeovers.

f. More debt vs. equity: Measures designed to get multinational corporations to invest more by debt inflow than equity.

g. Limit grants to subsidiaries: Reduce government grants to foreign-owned firms for new plants, research, etc.

h. Expand key sectors: Expand key sector approach to foreign investment policy to cover more industries or additional measures.

i. More control over subsidiaries: Canada should exert greater control over decisions and actions of foreign-owned firms.

j. Improve behavior of subsidiaries: The performance of foreign-owned firms should be better directed to serve Canadian interests.

k. Agency to monitor behavior: A government unit should be created to collect information about foreign-owned firms and to direct actions to improve their behavior.

l. Canadian majority on boards of directors: Requirement that Canadian citizens compose the majority of all corporate boards.

m. Require more financial disclosure: Require that foreign-owned firms report more fully on their operations.

n. More exports by subsidiaries: Foreign-owned firms should increase their exports from Canada.

o. More R&D subsidiaries: Foreign-owned firms should do more research in Canada.

p. Give information on plant shutdowns: Firms should be required to give notice and information before shutting down plants.

q. Obey Canadian laws: Foreign-owned firms should be required to obey Canadian laws.

r. Avoid extraterritorial law application: Measures to ensure that laws of foreign countries do not govern actions of foreign-owned firms in Canada.

s. Develop multinational control of multinational corporations: Encourage the development of approaches to controlling multinational firms by joint action of many host countries.

Industrial Strategy

a. Encourage development of Canadian firms: General policy of fostering Canadian-owned firms to build up nationally owned sector relative to the foreign-owned portion.

b. Expand public sector: Accomplishment of "a" by government-owned industry.

c. Increase Canadian investment in industry: Measures to increase the investment of Canadian capital in equities of Canadian firms: General —Tax and other devices affecting investment by general public. By financial institutions—Incentives and changes in legal requirements affecting pension funds and other institutions.

d. Divert outflow of capital for domestic use: Exchange controls or other measures to check outflow of investment funds so that they will be used for Canadian development.

e. Greater use of Industrial Development Bank: Increasing investment by expanding IDB activity.

f. Create Canada Development Corporation: Advocacy of CDC, which was set up in 1971. Note that concepts of its role differed between Liberals and NDP.

g. Create Capital Resource Fund: Investment unit proposed by NDP.

h. Pick special fields for industrial development: The "special niche" concept (see Chapter 4) that Canada should concentrate development in a few fields of particular capability or future promise.

i. Rationalization: Rationalizing industry for greater efficiency either by consolidating companies within Canada or on a continental basis with Canadian plants specializing in products with open access to U.S. market.

j. Increased R&D: Government support for greater research and development by Canadian firms.

k. Foster entrepreneurship and management: Build up the capabilities of Canadian businessmen.

l. Establish "buy Canadian" rules: Measures to favor products made in Canada in procurement.

m. Develop Canadian multinational corporations: Foster the expansion of Canadian firms to become multinational corporations.

n. Resources: More processing in Canada—Requirements that a greater degree of processing of raw materials be done in Canada.

Avoid continental energy policy—Do not enter into long-term commitments with the United States for export of energy resources.

Index

Adams Iron Ore Mine, 174
Adler-Karlsson, Gunnar, 145
AFL-CIO, 52
Agricultural equipment, 115
Aircraft, ownership, 170
Alberta, 76, 88, 89, 115, 116, 141
Alcan, 154
Arctic pipeline, 97, 164
Automotive Trade Agreement (Auto Pact), 21, 37, 111–13, 117, 140, 159

Bank Act of 1967, 101, 140, 171–72
Bank of Canada, 158
Banks, 42, 101, 140, 155, 171–72
Barford, Ralph, 102
Beigie, Carl, 34, 78, 139
Bell, Joel, 144
Bennett, W. A. C., 46
Benson, Edgar, 66
Biddell, J. L., 124
Boards of directors, composition, 54, 60, 61, 141, 152, 163, 164, 169, 170, 171, 176, 183, 184, 185
Bomarc missiles, 64
Britain, attitudes toward foreign investment, 14, 50

British Columbia, attitudes and policies, 38, 142
Broadcasting Act, 169
Burke-Hartke bill, 52
Businessmen, attitudes, 48

Campbell, A. B., 46
Canada Corporations Act, 151, 172, 179
Canada Development Corporation, 11, 54, 60–61, 99–100, 109, 153, 179, 182, 183, 185–87
Canadian-American Committee, 67, 118, 124
Canadian Broadcasting Corporation, 10, 30
Canadian Development Fund, 185
Canadian Labour Congress, 51, 52
Canadian National Energy Board, 88
Capital, 6, 7, 8, 53, 61, 89, 96–102
Capital Resources Fund, 185
China, trade with, 158
Committee for an Independent Canada, 27, 41–43, 48, 55, 59, 60, 63, 113, 145, 154, 161, 164, 165, 183
Communications media, 10, 155

Conference Board of Canada, 102
Connally, John, 16
Continentalism, 46, 87, 98, 115, 123
Control Data Corporation, 118
Cordell, Arthur, 94, 96
Corporations and Labour Union Returns Act, 151, 170
Crean, John, 159
Culture, Canadian, 29

Danforth, H. W., 123
Davey Committee, 48, 68
Davis, William G., 58, 60, 77, 78, 139, 162
Defense Production Sharing Program, 108, 110–111
de Haviland, 107
Dennison Mines, 11, 146
Deutsch, John, 21
Diefenbaker, John, 57, 64
Dobell, Peter, 46
Domestic International Sales Corporation (DISC), 16, 33, 52, 66
Douglas, T. C., 179, 185, 186, 187
Dow Chemical, Limited, 116
Drew, George, 15
Duerr, Michael G., 135
du Pont of Canada, 116, 120

Eastman, H. C. M., 94
Economic Council of Canada, 83, 91, 97, 108, 122
Economist (London), 96
Education, foreign impact on, 30
Elections, 1972, 63
Employment, 38, 82, 91, 117, 127, 161, 163, 183
Energy policy, 87, 113, 178
Entrepreneurship, 102–3
Esso, 116
European Economic Community, 104
Exchange rate, 86, 104
Exports, 81, 103–5, 115, 123, 138, 143, 151, 175, 179
Extraterritorial application of laws, 158–59, 183

Fairweather, Gordon, 59–60, 183, 184
Fayerweather, John, 22

Finance, 10, 155
Financial disclosure, 54, 60, 61, 151, 169, 176, 179, 182, 184
First National City Bank of New York, 101, 140, 172
Ford Motor Company, 23, 111, 158
Foreign Investment Review Agency, 149, 185
Foreign Investment Review bill, 3, 163, 173–74
Foreign Takeovers Review bill, 3, 51, 59, 73, 78, 162, 173, 181, 187
France, attitudes toward foreign investment, 14, 50

Gallup polls, 24
Galt, U.S.A., 47, 99, 138
Gas, natural, exports, 88
GATT, 81, 121
General Electric Company, 110
General Investment Corporation (Quebec), 99
Gerace, Mary C., 14, 20, 39
Gillespie, Alastair, 93, 148, 163, 165, 180
Gillies, James, 27, 154
Gordon, Walter, 40, 41, 43, 140, 143, 161, 170, 172
Gordon Report, 3, 9, 15, 20, 169
Government-business relations, 73–75
Government officials, attitudes, 49
Grant, George, 29, 36, 49, 50, 68, 166
Gray, Herb, 3, 180
Gray Report, 3, 15, 20, 34, 59, 74, 77, 130, 136, 139, 141, 142, 143, 151, 152, 161, 173, 180
Greene, J. J., 87, 180
Grosart, Allister, 46–47
Gulf Oil Company, 116

Hamilton, Alvin, 87
Home Oil Company, 11, 146
Hurtig, Mel, 27, 63, 64

Immigration, 96
Industrial Development Bank, 11, 54, 61, 182
Industry councils, 42, 127
Industry, Trade and Commerce, Department of, 129, 130

Insurance companies, 156, 170
Interest Equalization Tax, 16
International Business Machines Corporation, 118
International Chamber of Commerce, Canadian Council, 160
International Nickel Company, 154
Investment
  British, 6
  foreign, 5, 9, 14, 21
  foreign, control effects, 20, 25, 49, 113, 142–50, 169, 183
  foreign, cultural effects, 20, 25
  foreign, economic effects, 20, 25, 143
  foreign, review, 9
  United States, 5
  restrictions, domestic, 100
Investment Companies Act, 172, 179
Investment houses, 11, 48, 77, 101, 140, 141, 155, 174

Kaplan, Robert, 27, 59, 64
Kierans, Eric, 50, 89, 91, 119
Key sector policy, 10–11, 53–54, 62, 155–58, 173, 182, 184

Labor leaders, attitudes, 50
Lambert, Adrien, 86
Lambert, Marcel, 27, 60, 63, 64, 162
Lamontagne, Maurice, 93, 95, 103, 125–28
Land, ownership and leasing, 170, 171
Laxer, James, 40
Lewis, David, 21, 58, 185, 186, 187
Lewis, Stephen, 99
Liberal Party, 20, 27, 35, 40, 52–65, 91, 142, 161, 164, 178–81
Lithwick, N. H., 133
Litvak, I. A., 134, 168
Loan and trust companies, 170–71, 172, 174
Loans to foreign-owned firms, 153, 174, 186

Macdonald, Donald S., 89, 181
Magazines, 30, 48, 140, 155, 171
Management, 102–3, 152

Manufacturing, 5, 80, 86, 90–124, 125
Maritime provinces, attitudes and policies, 38, 57, 77, 82, 90, 115
Martin, Paul, 179
Massey Ferguson, 103, 114, 115, 154, 155
Maule, C. J., 168
McClelland & Stewart, 174
McKie, Craig, 75
McLaughlin, W. Earle, 45–46
Meisel, John, 56
Mercantile Bank, 101, 140, 157, 171–72
Mergers, 109, 127
Merrill Lynch, Pierce, Fenner, & Smith, 141
Michelin, 115
Mining, 6
Montieth, J. W., 182
Movement for an Independent Socialist Canada, 40
Murray, J. Alex, 14, 20, 39

National Cash Register Company, 96, 118
Nationalism, 21, 27, 29, 31, 40, 64, 68, 86, 109, 113, 123, 137, 144
New Democratic Party, 20, 21, 40, 52–65, 91, 99, 161, 164, 165, 184–87
Newman, Peter, 41
Nixon, Richard M., 67, 86

O'Brian, Brice, 86
OECD Investment Code, 159
Ontario, attitudes and policies, 23, 38, 48, 57, 76, 77, 115, 141, 152, 153, 174
Ontario Business Corporations Act, 174
Ontario Development Corporation, 174
Ontario Employment Standards Act, 149
Ontario Select Committee on Economic and Cultural Nationalism, 174
Ownership, 113, 142–50, 164, 169, 170, 172, 173, 176, 182, 183, 185, 186

Pearson, Lester, 35, 161, 170

Penner, Stephen, 41
Pepin, Jean-Luc, 95, 107, 112, 116, 129, 132, 144, 179, 181
Perry, Robert, 47
Petrochemicals, 115–17
Petroleum, 6, 38, 76, 89, 171
Plant shutdowns, 149, 187
Polymer Limited, 99, 116, 117
Porter, John, 55, 74
Prairie provinces, attitudes and policies, 38, 58
Pricing, intercorporate, 113–14
Product specialization, 105–8, 179
Progressive Conservative Party, 20, 27, 52–65, 152, 161, 164, 182–84
Property rights, 10, 140
Provincial governments, 21, 58, 60, 76–78, 129, 183
Publishing, 141, 155, 157, 174

Quebec, attitudes and policies, 38, 77, 82, 115

Rationalization, 108–19, 175, 179
Raynauld, Andre, 46
RCA, 93, 110
Reader's Digest, 48, 140, 157, 171
Regenstreiff, Peter, 26
Regional economic development, 128
Research and development, 92–96, 119, 126, 138, 143, 151, 153, 179, 183
Resources, natural, 5, 73, 80, 84–90, 104, 125, 180, 183, 187
Richardson, R. J., 120
Robinson, R. D., 168
Rock, Raymond, 20
Rotstein, Abraham, 41, 75, 145

Safarian, A. E., 133
Saltsman, Max, 20, 23, 186
Sarnia Olefins and Aromatics Project (SOAP), 116, 117
Schreyer, Edward, 58
Science Council of Canada, 93, 94, 98, 99, 130, 136
Senate Committee on Science Policy, 93, 118, 125
Sharp, Mitchell, 35, 67, 122, 123, 152, 159, 181
Short takeoff and landing (STOL) aircraft, 107

Simon Fraser University, 30
Smith, Dennis, 57
Stanfield, Robert L., 58, 60, 61, 63, 152, 179, 182, 183, 184
Sun Life Insurance Company, 156

Takeovers, review, 9, 21, 53, 146, 163–64, 173, 182, 183–84, 186
Tariffs, 6, 9, 73, 80, 109, 116, 119–22, 125
    Commonwealth preferences, 104
Taxation, 9, 11, 54, 63, 73, 76, 89, 91, 100, 114, 153, 170, 171
Television, 30, 155, 169
Time, 48, 140, 157, 171
Tires, 115
Toronto *Daily Star,* 26, 39, 41, 98, 118
Trading with the Enemy Act, U.S., 158
Trudeau, Pierre Elliot, 21, 27, 31, 35, 36, 50, 64, 67, 68, 76, 78, 83, 105, 146, 152, 161, 165, 179, 180–81
Truncated firm, 34
Turner, John N., 159

Unions, labor, 42, 50–52
United Aircraft Company, 107
United States
    Canadian relations with, 35, 46–47, 57, 66–68, 122
    economic policies, 15, 137
    labor protectionism, 52, 66, 114

Venturetek, 99
Vernon, Raymond, 139
Vietnam War, 15, 67
Volcker, Paul, 67

Waffle Group, 40, 51, 55, 185
Wahn, Ian, 59
Wahn Report, 111, 136, 143, 159, 172, 180, 186
Watkins, Melville, 40
Watkins Report, 3, 9, 20, 172, 179, 185
Winters, Robert, 12, 171, 175–76, 178–79
Winters Guidelines, 12, 143, 146, 151, 175–76, 178
World Bank Convention on Investment Disputes, 160